DAYS OF LAVENDER

A Chronicle of Bloom & burn

BY WALTER RED

LEGACY REBIRTH HARDCOVER EDITION

... GHOST WRITTEN • SELF FORGED • SFD • STILL HERE ...

© 2025 Walter Red Books LLC. All rights reserved.

No part of this publication may be reproduced, distributed, or transmitted

in any form or by any means, including photocopying, recording, or other

electronic or mechanical methods, without the prior written permission of

the publisher, except in the case of brief quotations embodied in critical

reviews and certain other noncommercial uses permitted by copyright law.

First Edition ©2018 Ghost Writer Publishing

Rebirth Edition ©2025 Walter Red Books

Printed in the United States of America

ISBN:

Walter Red Books
www.walterredbooks.com

Other Titles by Walter Red

Death Songs — Ten Years

(Requiem for the First Cut)

Daddyland — The Complete Edition

(A Gospel of Desire & Ruin)

Analog Emotions — The Complete Edition

(A Voyage Through Dream & Debris)

Days of Lavender

(A Chronicle of Bloom and Burn)

The Whiskey Diaries

(Confessions at Closing Time)

Fresh Cuts — Artifacts from 2004–2009

(Juvenilia & Other Ghosts)

From the ruins of despair & ash.

Even flowers can bloom, beautiful & holy.

Table of Contents:

Rebirth

-Days of Lavender 2025 Edition

-Days of Lavender 2018 Original Pressing

The Bloom After Fire

-Academic Dissertation: On Softness, Survival, and Queer Renewal

Lavender In The Archive

Bonus Material

-Companion Zine

-Lost Poems

-Classroom Material

-Ghostbox Supplemental

The Vault

What if healing wasn't linear—but floral?

Archivist's Note:

Recovered from the Lavender Archives, restored under the soft light of Seattle.

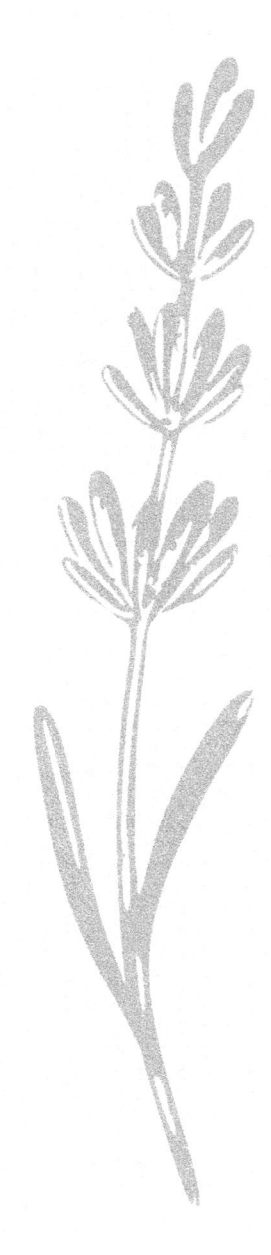

Dedication

For the days we bloomed quietly, then vanished.

For the people who made me soft.

For my Grandfather — I'll have the cribbage board ready.

SOME BLOOMS ONLY OPEN WHEN THE WORLD ISN'T WATCHING.

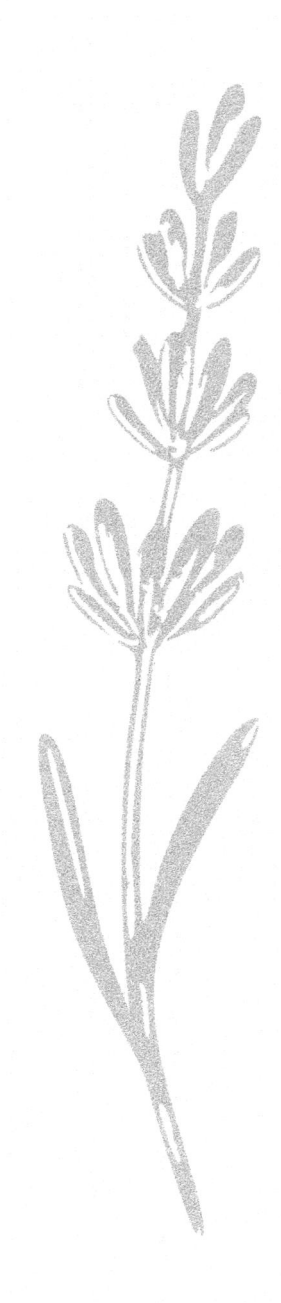

"The scent of lavender lingers long after the flower is gone."
— Pierre-Joseph Redouté

ラベンダー

"If you must know anything, know that the hardest task is to live only once."
—Ocean Vuong, Night Sky with Exit Wounds

EVERY BREATH IS A SEED DECIDING TO STAY.

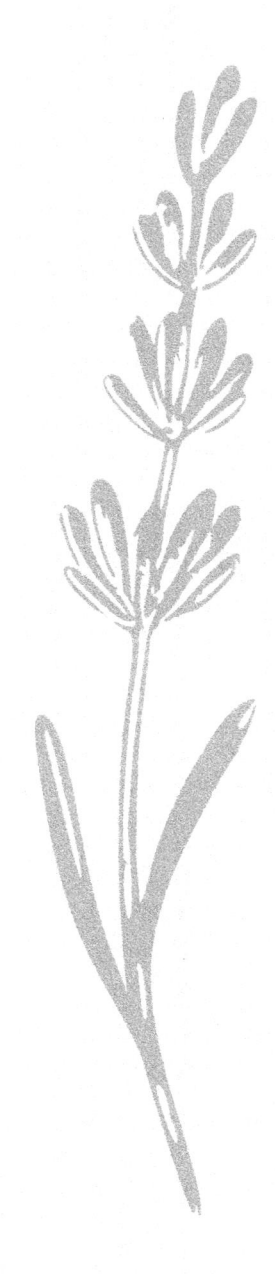

Preface / Author's Note:

There are books written out of survival, and then there are books written out of returning.
Days of Lavender began in a rented room with peeling paint, a window that never opened all the way, and a boy who didn't know softness could be something worth keeping.

I didn't mean for this book to bloom after a funeral, but that's what lavender does—it finds the cracks and grows anyway. These poems are what came after the silence: not an apology, but a pulse.

Every poem here is a kind of offering: to the friends who stayed, the ghosts who listened, the stranger who smiled at the right time. It's an act of faith to stay gentle in a world that keeps hardening, but I've learned that softness is the bravest thing we can become.

This is my return to color, to scent, to the small miracles of being alive.

— *Walter Red*
Seattle, Fall 2025

Invocation

I came here with soil beneath my nails.
With a name half-buried and a heart that still hummed
beneath the dirt.
I knelt where the house once stood, and found the first
green thread.

The earth spoke quietly:
grow again.

Every word I plant here is a return
Every scent is a memory turned soft.

I light a match for the ones who stayed,
pour water for the ones who couldn't,
whisper air into the names I forgot,
and rest my hand against the earth that remembers us both.

This is how I return.

Not as the ghost from Death Songs,
not as the confessor from Daddyland,
but as the boy who learned that even ruin smells like
lavender when the rain begins.

Let what was buried rise again in color.
Let the scent carry forward.

The Days of Orchids
(Death)

Threshold Invocation — Earth

"Every death of love is compost for the next bloom."

Lay your hand upon the soil and remember your name.
The roots know the syllables you forgot.
Breathe until the ground answers.

What I bury, I keep alive.

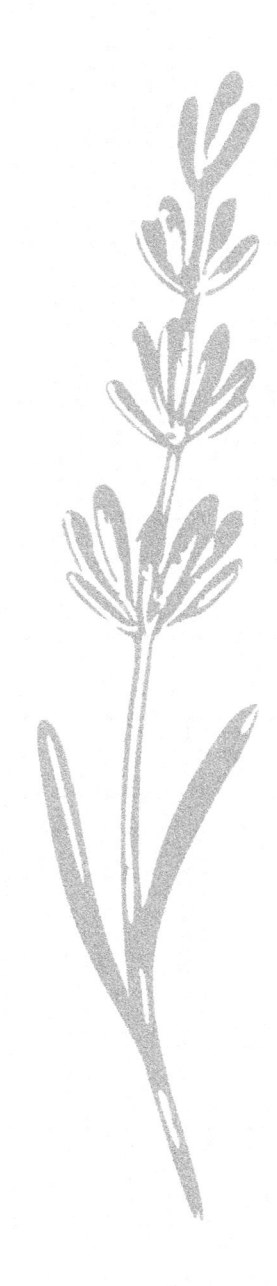

LAVENDER ARRIVES IN A HOUSE WITHOUT WINDOWS

It didn't knock. It slipped in like weather—
a soft insistence along the floorboards,
dust glittering as if the day had been polished from within.

I thought ruin was my only furniture.
But the scent was patient, old as kitchens and prayers.
It circled the room, counted every quiet, and said:

Hold still. I am here to make the empty gentler.

Some griefs are carpenters.
They remove what can't be carried up the stairs.
They leave a table you can finally sit at,
even if it wobbles when you breathe.

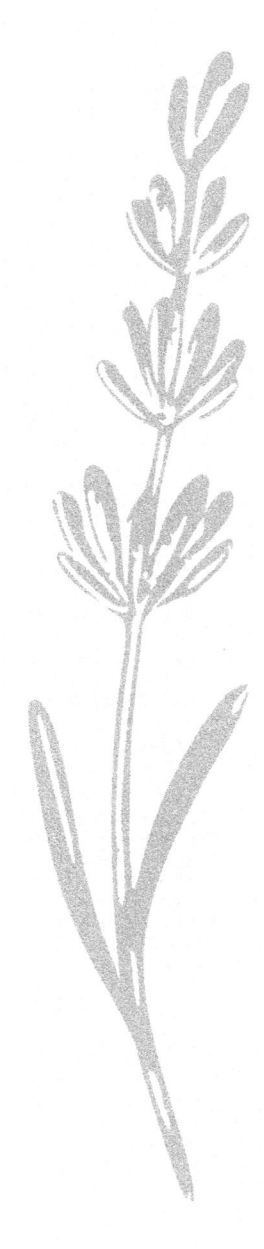

THE CUP WE KEPT FILLING

We poured our worrisome nights into a single cup—
juniper shadows, rosemary thunder, a lime bitten to blood.
It never overflowed. It only blurred the rim.

There are vessels shaped like a promise and vessels shaped like a door.
We chose the promise again and again,
and wondered why the room never changed.

I set the cup in the sink, let the faucet speak.
Water learned my name faster than I did.
When the glass cleared, a small sky remained.

I drank it. It tasted like windows.

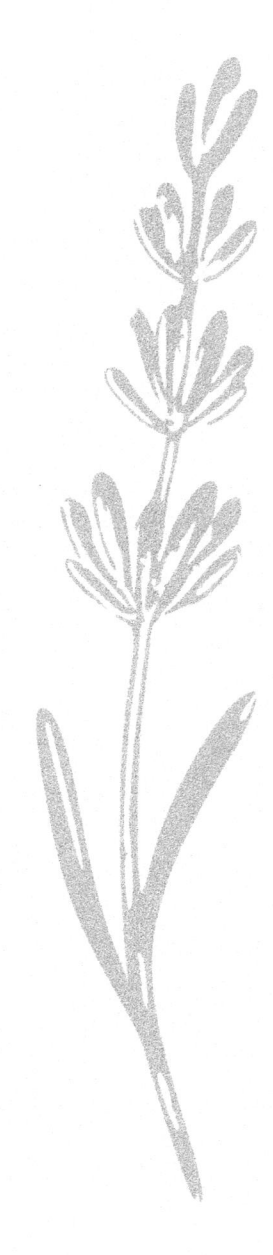

JEALOUSY IS A NARROW STREET

How sharp we became in the narrow!
Even our kindness had corners.
We tried to pass without scraping the paint,
tried to hold our mouths like unlit matches.

A city of us existed in a single breath.
Listen: tires hiss after rain, a siren threads the block,
two boys carry a new mattress up three flights
and laugh when it doesn't fit the door.

I was the alley that kept the echo.
You were the echo that learned to fold itself small.
We met in the wall we built and finally understood its height.

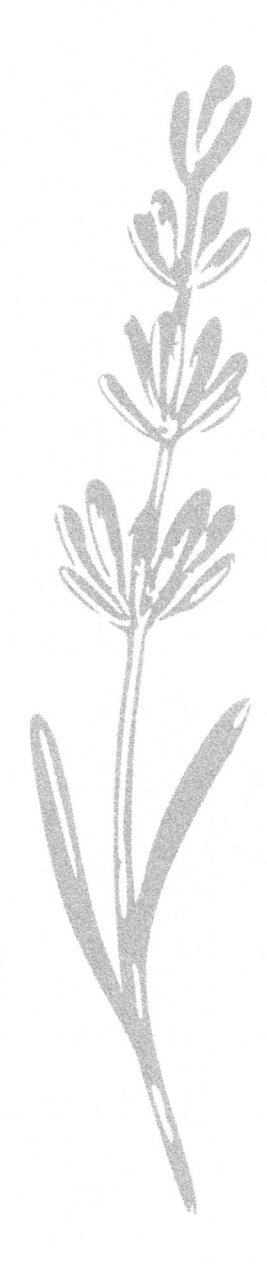

A BRIEF HISTORY OF THE BODY (AS A ROOM)

    There was an evening I called myself home
and meant it.
I dusted the mantle. I put the photographs upright.
I told the mirror thank you for keeping the wrong light.

    If I touched the wall, a pulse answered.
Not mine—ours. The room and I learning to share a breath.
When the house sighed, the curtains applauded.
Even the floor forgave my pacing.

    "Stay," the lamp said without words, and I stayed.
"Sleep," said the quiet, and I slept.
I woke to lavender kneeling at the door.

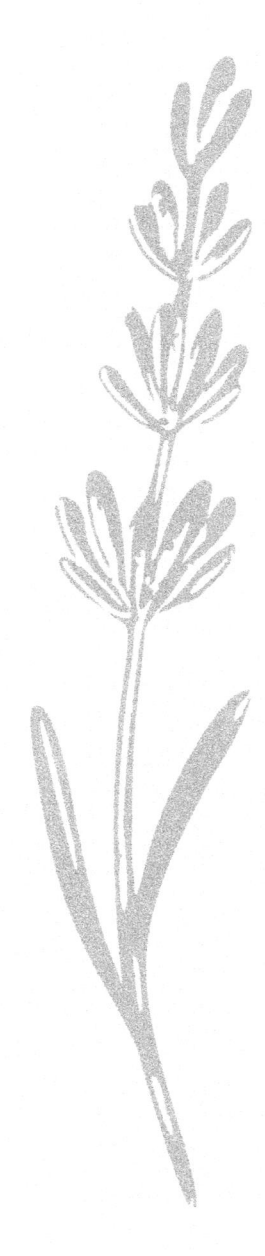

FIELD NOTE: AFTER THE STORM, COUNTING

1 sparrow in the gutter,
2 receipts stuck together,
3 rings on the table from the same sweating glass,
4 questions that keep their feet under the bed,
5 breaths taken before the phone was answered,
6 months of turning the calendar without writing a single name,
7 mornings when the light remembered me,
8 seeds found under the porch, patient as saints,
9 times I thought silence would break me,
10 times it made a path instead.

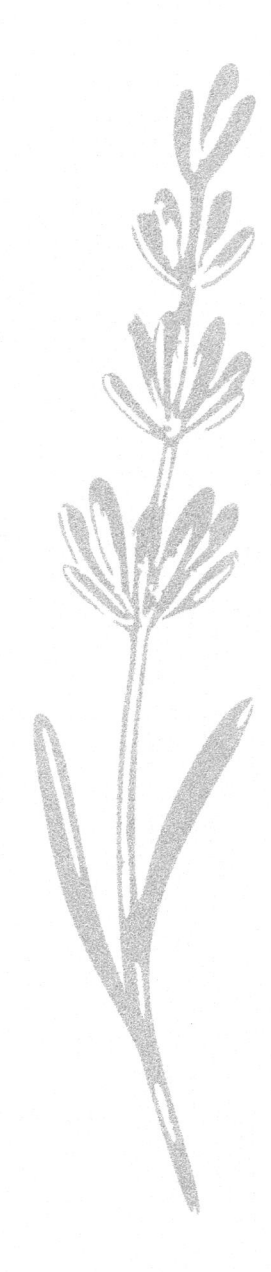

YOUR EYES WERE DAGGERS / I LEARNED TO SEW

Yes, the gaze can cut—
but a thread is also sharp, and gentler.

I pricked my thumb to stitch the torn place,
watched a small bead of red think itself a planet,
then fall back into the gravity of skin.

We mended what would let us.
We named the rest "archive."

There is no violence in a seam, only patience.
Even the needle bows its head to pass.

WHITE ROOMS, QUIET ROOMS

There were rooms where the air was an endless page.
We wrote our names and they lifted like birds.
We wrote our fear and it slept in the margin.

When night snowed on the city, I listened for thawing.
Some windows keep their winter longer than others.
I warmed mine with breath until it kissed back.

Softness is weather too.
It arrives, it lingers, it leaves a note.
I folded the note into a small boat and floated it in a basin of light.

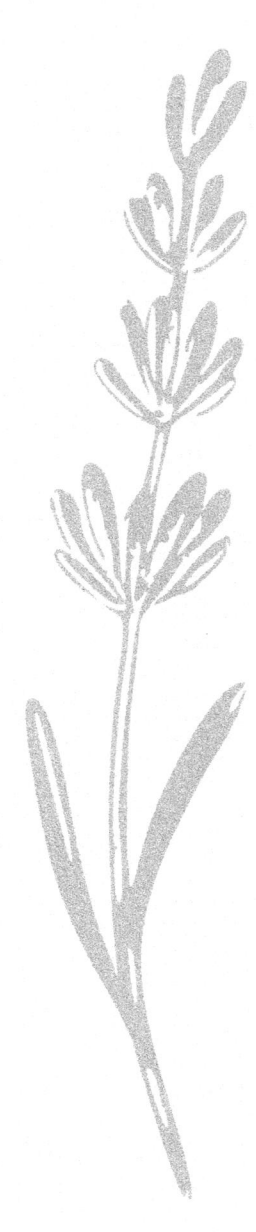

LETTER I NEVER SENT (ICE CREAM ON A MONDAY)

    You made mint taste like a choice.
We stood under a sky that had the good sense to stay uncomplicated.
I laughed with my whole mouth.

    I wanted to tell you that forgiveness has a temperature.
That your hand near mine made the air remember July.
That the spoon was a crescent moon and I almost wished.

    Instead, I kept the napkin with the ring of your glass.
It dried into a small planet I visit when the night needs a door.

ORNITHOLOGY OF GRIEF

In the mornings I studied the black birds.
Not crows, not ravens—just the ones that refuse to be metaphor
unless you've earned it.

They taught me how to stand on wet branches,
how to take off without proof of land,
how to return with nothing but a rumor of the sea.

I stopped asking for omens and asked for directions.
They pointed at the ground.

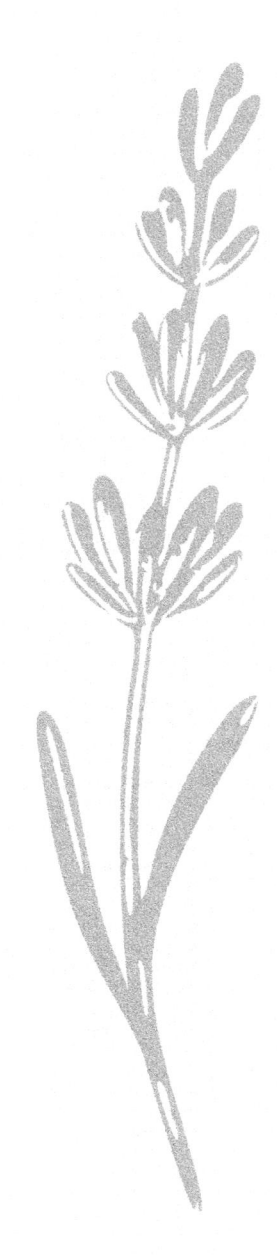

MUSEUM OF NEARLY

The exhibit is quiet.
Here are the glasses we almost raised, the coat you almost forgot, the phone call almost answered on the first ring.
Here is a room of closed mouths practicing a different alphabet.

A guard nods me past the velvet rope.
"Touch what you need," he says.
I lay my palm on a small plaque:

NEARLY IS A DOOR WITH ITS HINGES ON THE INSIDE.

When I push, something opens behind me.

SLOW WEATHER (I)

What if we measured healing by rainfall, not clocks.
What if an afternoon could be a year, if the window understood.
What if the sky remembered my first name and called it back, softly,
until my mouth answered with the right shape.

I don't want a miracle.
I want the weather to keep its promise.

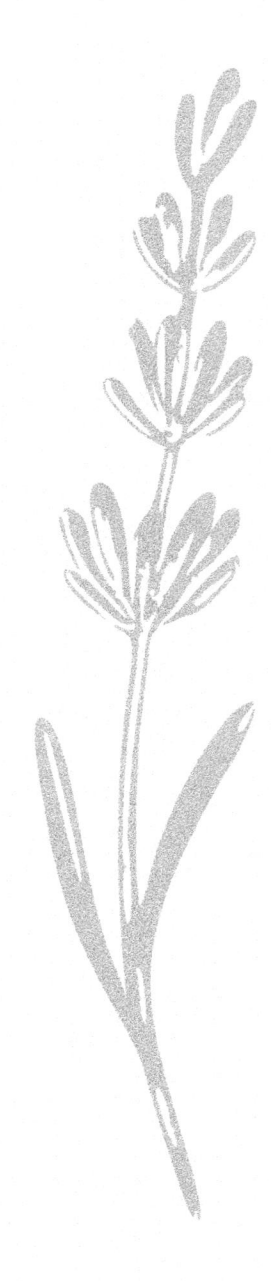

INVENTORY AFTER THE LEAVING

One shirt that knows August.
Three books that smell like rooms I used to be.
A jar of coins, a feather, a map with two cities circled too hard.

I kept the softest things:
the laugh you left on the stairwell,
the kindness the neighbor slid under the door,
the way the street-lamps made saints of puddles.

I threw away the instructions for staying the same.

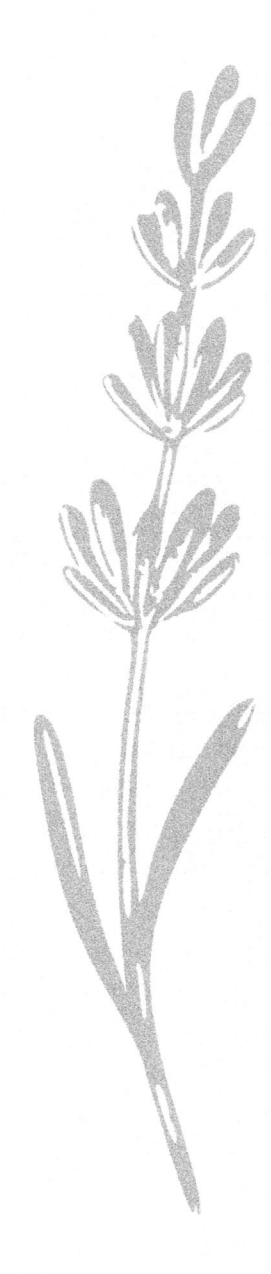

PETITION TO THE ROOT

Beneath the house, the ground holds an alphabet older than my mouth.
I write my request on my bones and knock once.

Teach me to be quiet without leaving.
Teach me to be still without stopping.
Teach me to carry rain.

The answer is a thrum.
It sounds like a throat deciding to sing.

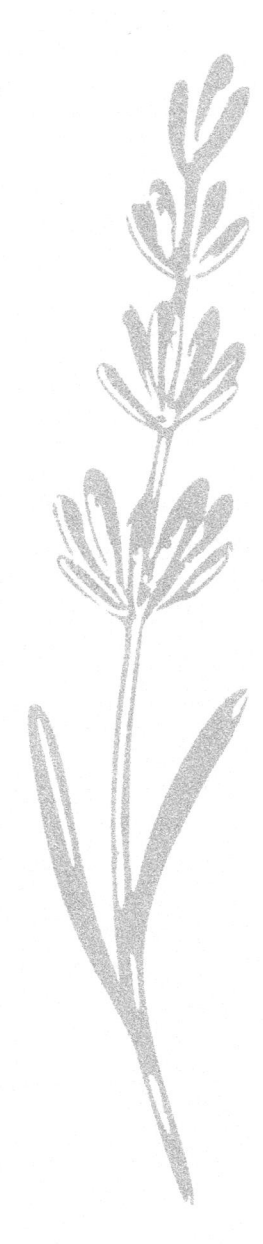

WHERE WE PUT THE SHARP THINGS

There is a drawer for what could cut the day.
We line it in linen. We bless it with ordinary light.
We open it with both hands and close it gently.

The sharp things aren't evil.
They simply do their job too well.

I keep a single thorn beside the spoons as proof
that roses make their own arguments.

Some evenings I hold it long enough to listen,
then return it to its small kingdom of mercy.

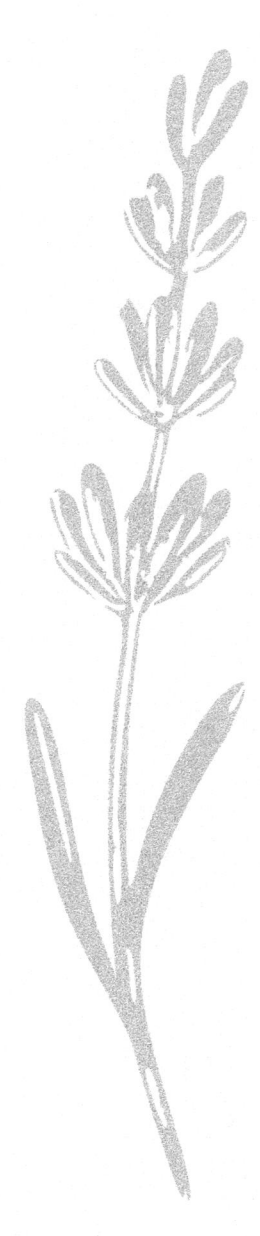

THE COLOR OF QUIET

It is not white.
It is the gray of rain-warmed sidewalks,
the green of a leaf reconsidering,
the deep night-blue a window keeps when it chooses you back.

Quiet has weight.
It sits on the pillow beside you and doesn't ask for anything.
It learns the shape of your shoulder and says stay.

I stayed.

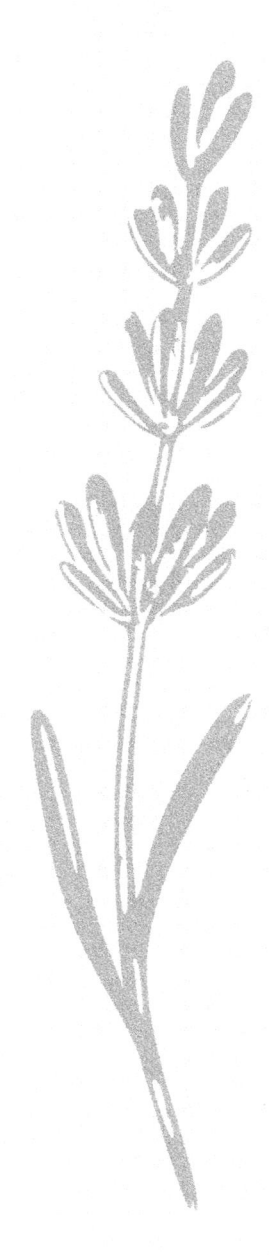

STILL LIFE WITH LANTERN

A table. A bowl of ordinary pears.
A lantern whose wick remembers rivers.

I lift the glass. The flame listens to my breath,
leans, returns, becomes itself again.

In another life I would have asked the light a thousand questions.
In this one I thank it and try to deserve the answer.

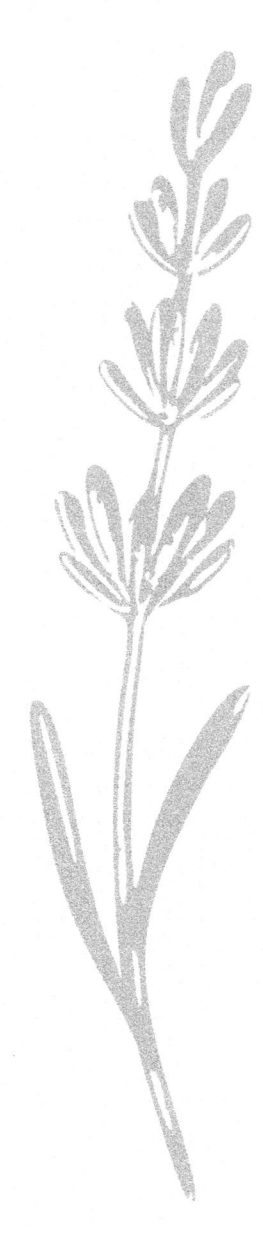

SLOW WEATHER (II)

How merciful, to measure by blossoms.
The tree outside fails spectacularly into pink
and no one calls it failure.

I stand below the storm of petals and become a map of soft landfalls.
Every touch is a syllable. Every syllable, a reason to keep learning my name.

Lavender in the air.
A boy I used to be nods from the past and lets me go.

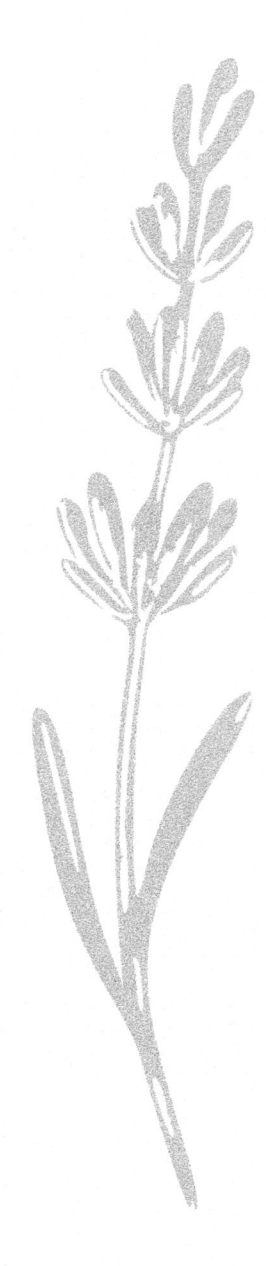

THE PROMISE WE COULD KEEP

We could not keep each other—
so we kept the door.

We could not keep the morning—
so we kept the cup it blessed.

We could not keep the boy—
so we kept his laughter,
and taught it to find us in quiet rooms.

What remains is not less.
It is the shape of a hand made ready to hold what's next.

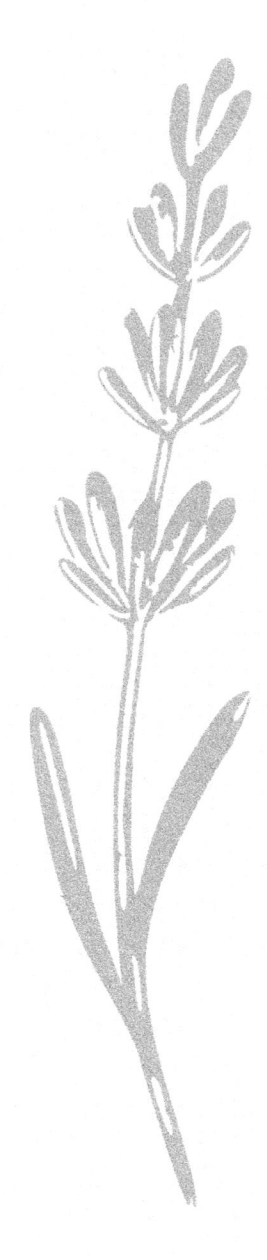

ARCHIVIST'S NOTE ON ORCHIDS

Orchids do not punish.
They wait.
They require a different kind of listening.

This section was recovered with soil under the fingernails.
Left as evidence.
Filed as instruction.

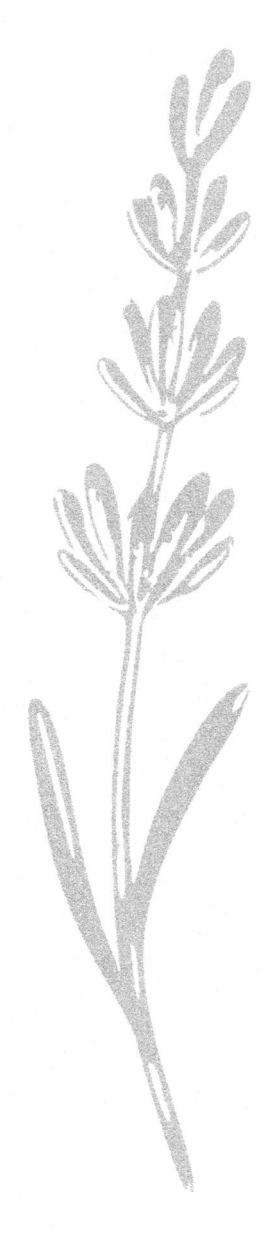

CLOSING THE EARTHWORK

I put the room back as if love were a visitor due any minute.
I smooth the coverlet, open a window, straighten the glass.

A scent moves through, unafraid of being named.
I press my palm to the floor and feel the answering warmth.

When I rise, the door is lighter in my hand.

BENEATH THE HOUSE, THE ROOTS KEEP THEIR OWN GOSPEL.
I KNEEL IN DUST, WHISPERING EVERY NAME I BURIED.
THE EARTH ANSWERS SOFTLY:
CHILD OF ROT, YOU ARE STILL BECOMING

"The ground remembers what the heart forgets."

THE RITUAL OF THE ROOT BENEATH THE HOUSE
▽

In every house there is a place that remembers.
Not the windows or the walls, but the quiet underneath—
where water drips slow, where roots find the warmth of what's been lost.

This is where the ritual begins.

Bring a single object that still hums with your name: a photograph, a torn sleeve, a scent of summer.
Place it on the floor and kneel.

You will feel the house listening.

Light a candle and trace its smoke along the edges of the room.
Let the ash fall onto the floorboards—this is your first language.

When the flame is out, press your hand to the earth beneath the boards.
Imagine the roots turning toward your pulse.

Stay there until you feel the thrum of something older than memory.
That is the root.
It knows what to hold and what to let go.

Rise slowly.
The floor will creak; the world will breathe.

Above you, the scent of lavender begins to spread.
You have not left the house.
You have *become* it.

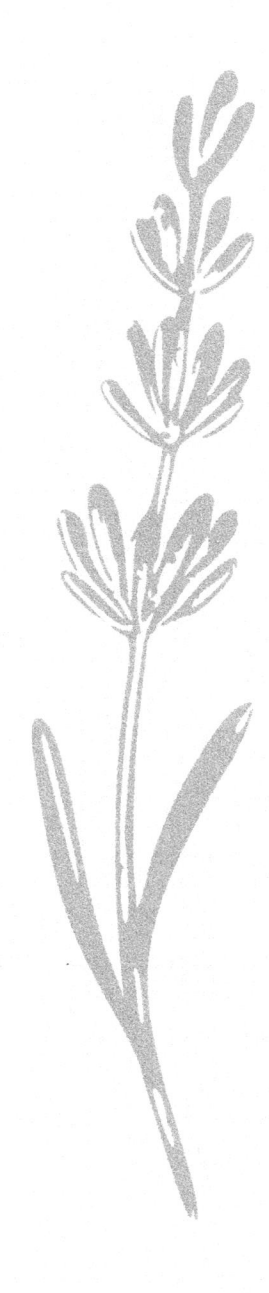

ARCHIVIST ENTRY: BETWEEN EARTH AND WATER

The soil has been turned; now the water comes.
What was buried begins to breathe.
The roots whisper that memory has had its say—
and so, the basin fills.

We enter not as mourners,
but as those who have washed their hands in forgiveness
and found the scent still clinging.

This is the passage from rot to rain.
From holding the ground too tightly,
to letting it hold us back.

When you are ready, lean over the vessel.
The reflection that greets you is not who you were,
but who remained after the storm.

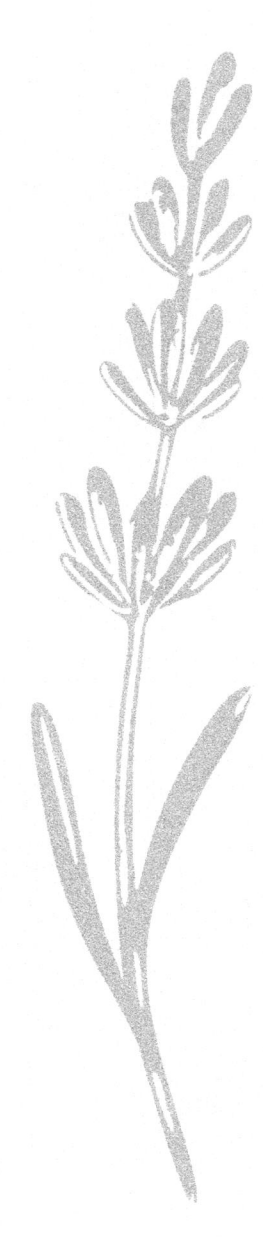

Beneath the house, the roots keep their own gospel.

I kneel in dust, whispering every name I buried.

The earth answers softly: *child of rot, you are still becoming*

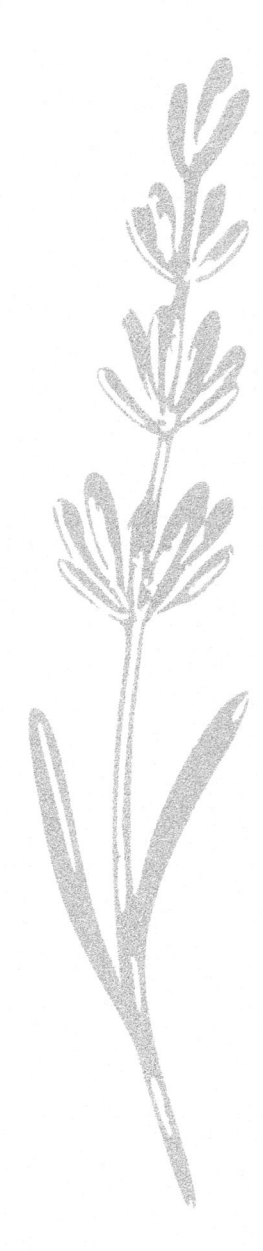

THE DAYS OF LAVENDER
(REBIRTH)

THRESHOLD INVOCATION — WATER

"THE SCENT OF LEARNING TO STOP FOR AIR."

Pour into the vessel and speak what you wish to cleanse.
Let the current unbraid what you once held tight.
When the water stills, look down—
even reflection is a form of forgiveness.

I *let the river remember me kindly.*

THE SOUND OF UNBRAIDING

Morning found me rinsing the night from my hands.
The faucet sang a small psalm of release.
Each drop struck porcelain like punctuation,
and the sentence ended softly.

The mirror fogged, forgiving its own clarity.
I traced a heart in the blur—
not to remember love, but to test the warmth of breath.

Everything blurred back into itself.
That was mercy.

FIELD NOTE: THE FIRST GREEN

There is a tremor between roots and bloom—
the instant the stem realizes it is no longer underground.
It stretches, dazed by light.
So do I.
I cup the sprout with dirt-rough palms.
It shakes, then steadies.
In its silence I hear a slow yes.

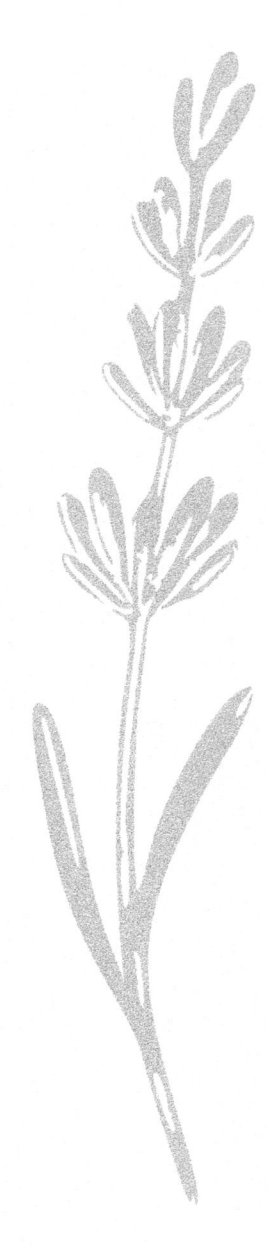

THE HOUSE LEARNS RAIN

    Water slipped through the cracks of the window frame
and did not apologize.
The sill darkened, the paint blistered.
I called it ruin once.
Now I call it listening.

    Every leak becomes a new throat.
Every drip learns your name if you stay long enough.

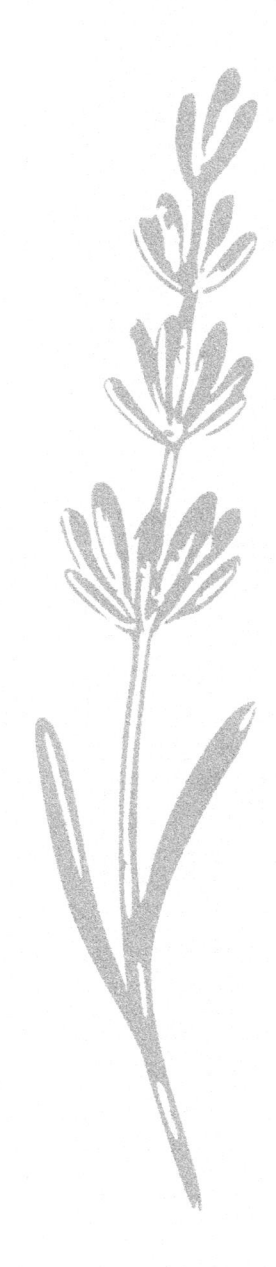

SELF-PORTRAIT AS VESSEL

    I fill easily.
I spill easier.
But the rim has learned patience.

    Inside me the river rehearses a hymn
for hands that tremble yet hold.
I am no longer afraid of overflow.

    The floorboards will understand.
They have survived worse floods.

THE TEMPERATURE OF FORGIVENESS

It isn't warm.
It is the exact cool of dusk water on wrist,
the place where pulse hides and returns.

When I forgave you,
it sounded like the sigh between two waves—
indistinguishable, endless.

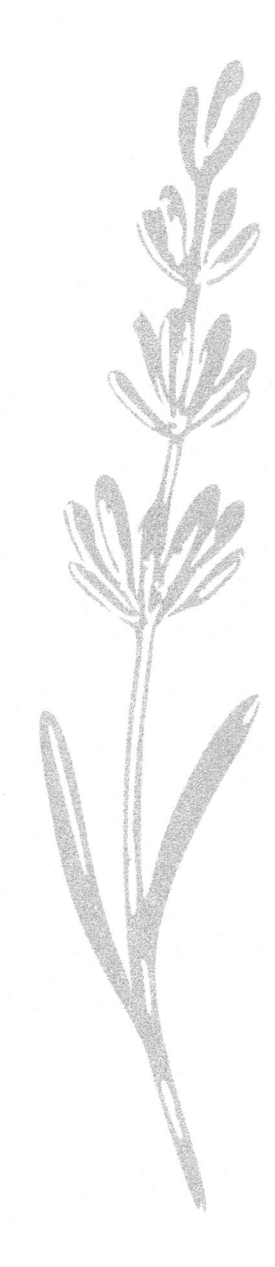

RELEARNING TOUCH

Steam rises.
The mirror breathes back.
You are standing in the threshold of every yes
I never dared to speak.

When you press your fingers to my collarbone,
the past exhales through me like a ghost
finally given direction.

I don't call it desire.
I call it current.

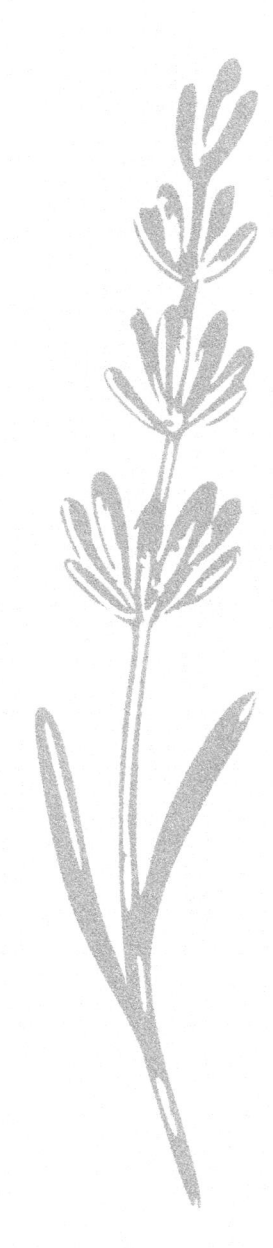

LAVENDER BOY (2025 VARIATION)

You weren't made of softness.
You carried it—
like a bruise carries color.

You weren't light.
You were what made me look toward it.

Your voice found me waist-deep in regret
and said, come up.
I surfaced blue-lipped, astonished at air.

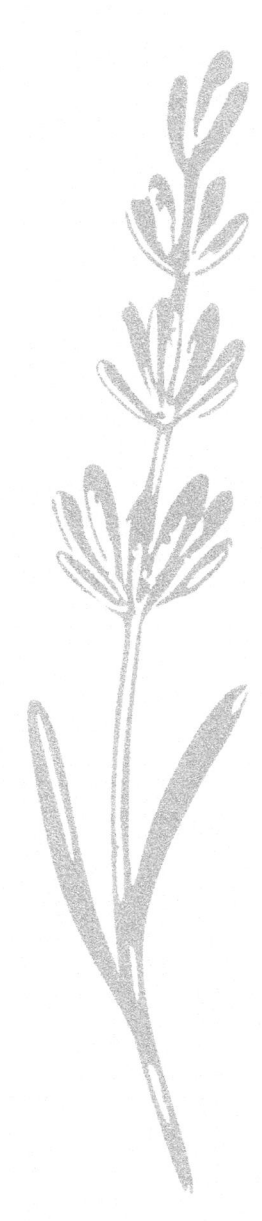

ICE CREAM ON A MONDAY (REPRISE)

We met again beneath an awning slick with rain.
You ordered mint; I chose the old ache—vanilla.
The cones leaned, the drizzle sweetened them into confession.

We didn't talk about the leaving.
We talked about flavors,
and somehow that was forgiveness.

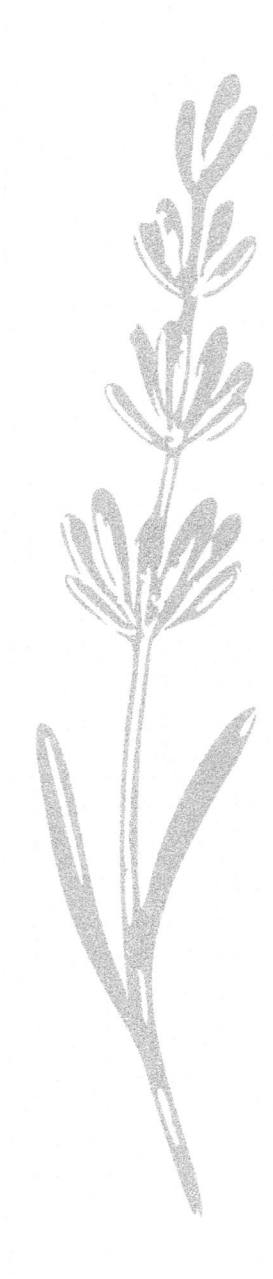

RITUAL OF RETURN

Step one: open the window.

Step two: set the cup by the sill.

Step three: let the rain fill it on its own.

    This is how I learn patience—
not from prayer, but from puddles.

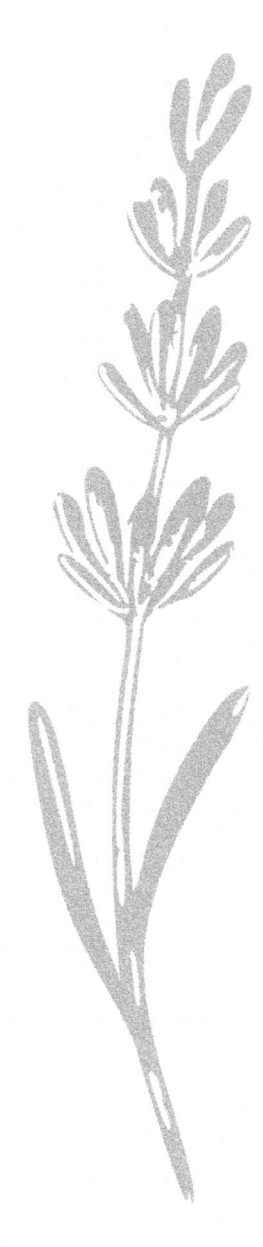

ANATOMY OF LIGHT

Every drop contains a window waiting to open.
I catch one on my tongue and taste the sky's intent.

If you listen closely, light has lungs.
It breathes through us when we remember to look up.

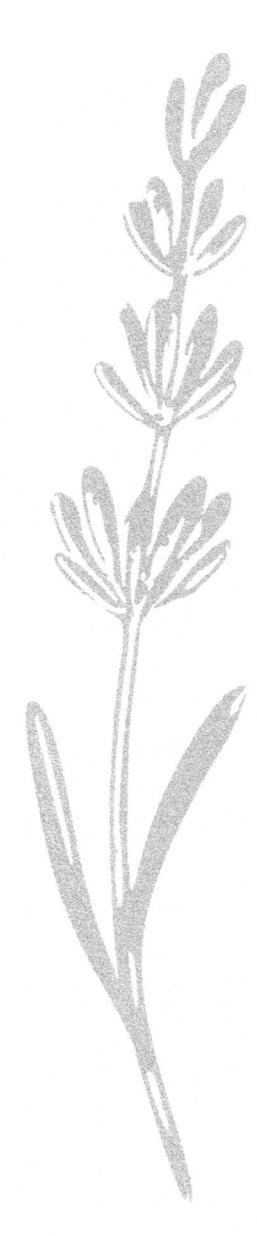

LETTER TO THE BODY AFTER HUNGER

You did not betray me.
You protected what you could until I learned to feed you kindness.

Now every mouthful is a benediction,
every touch a new language of thanks.

Eat. Drink. Stay.
We are finally home.

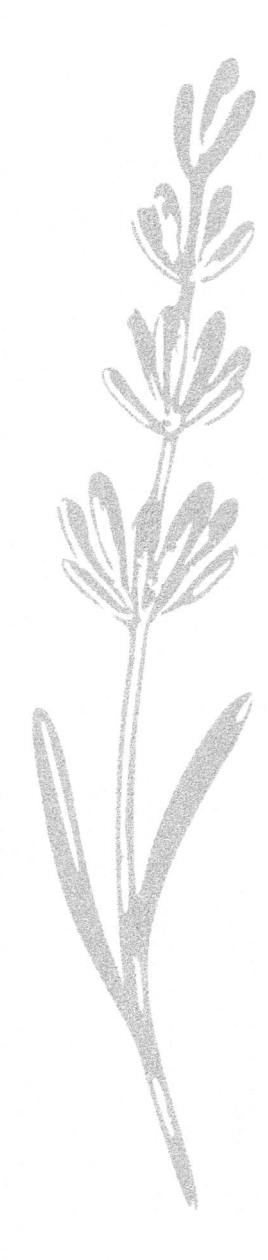

THE BASIN DREAM

I dream of a bowl that holds the moon without spilling. Inside it, the faces of everyone I have loved float like leaves.

When I wake, I fill the sink with water and see only myself. That is enough light for morning.

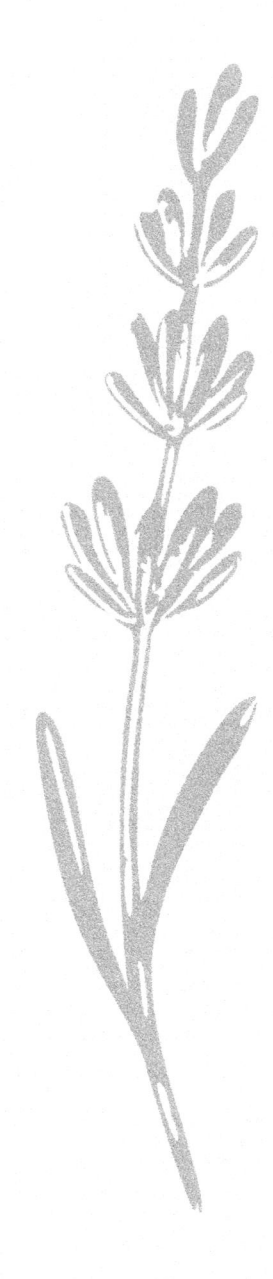

THE SCIENCE OF SOFTNESS

The heart is not a pump. It is a spring.
Compression makes music.
Release makes song.
 I press a hand to my chest and hear the first note again.
It sounds like forgiveness learning to pronounce its own name.

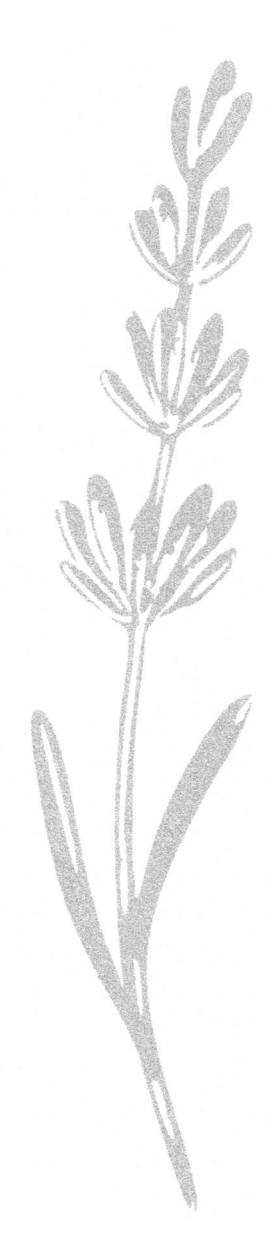

FIELD NOTE: THE RIVER UNDER THE FLOOR

While re-tiling the bathroom I found a trickle of sound—
a tiny current running beneath the house.

It carried words too small for speech.
I pressed my ear to the tile and understood enough:

keep going.

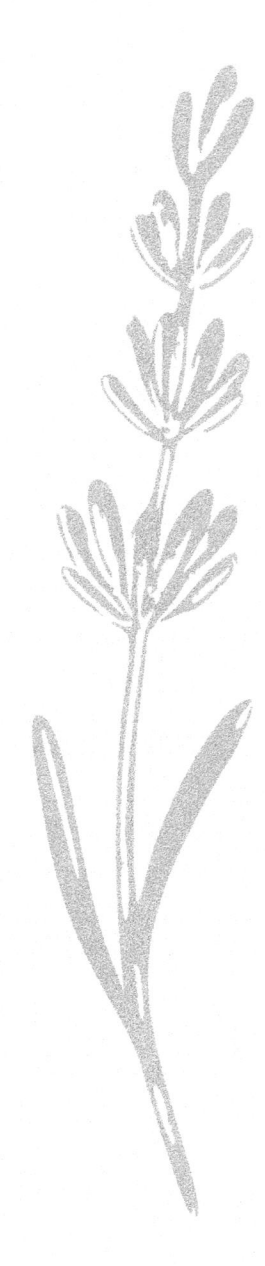

HYMN FOR THOSE WHO STAYED

You did not rescue me.
You waited while I learned how to surface.
That patience was its own miracle.

This poem is your thank you letter,
folded into water, unfolded by rain.

REBIRTH SCENE

The window open, curtain breathing,
skin smelling of rain and candle.

I walk into the light that forgives its own edges.
The room is a river.
I am its reflection, finally still.

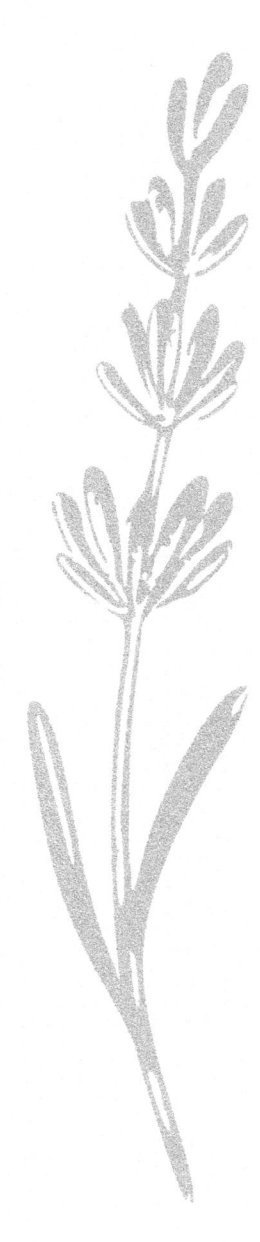

CLOSING INVOCATION — WATER

The river returns to itself, and so do I.
Hands drip clean.
The basin gleams with something beyond light—
the shape of continuance.

"Water does not ask to be held; it asks to hold."

THE EMBRACE – WATER RITUAL

Find a vessel deep enough to hold your reflection.
It doesn't matter if it's a bowl, a mirror, or the memory of someone's eyes.

Fill it with water.
Watch how the light moves inside it — a language made of ripples.

Dip your fingers in and name what you wish would soften.
The water will not keep your secrets, but it will make them gentler.

Submerge both hands.
Feel the temperature of forgiveness.

When you lift your palms, watch the drops fall back in.
This is how release looks: returning without vanishing.

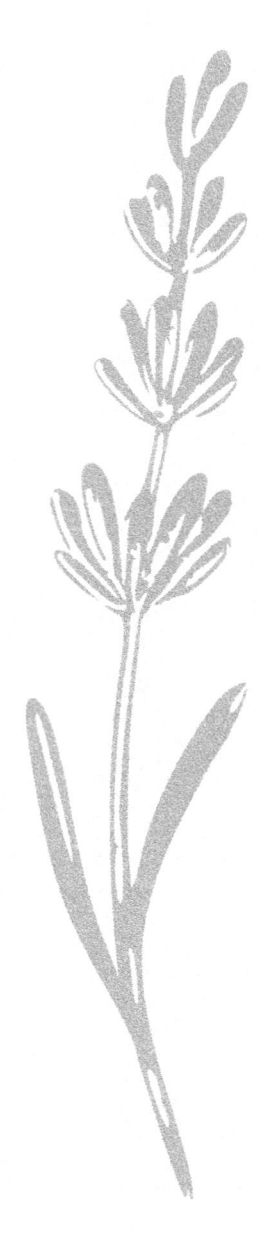

The basin overflows with light and memory.

Each drop carries a version of me that once drowned.

I let them go, one ripple at a time.

What stays behind is mercy.

THE DAYS OF SAGE (SEX)

Threshold Invocation — Fire

"Desire was never sin, only confession."

Strike the match.
Name your desire aloud.
Watch it tremble, certain.
Fire asks only truth of its fuel.

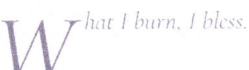hat I burn, I bless.

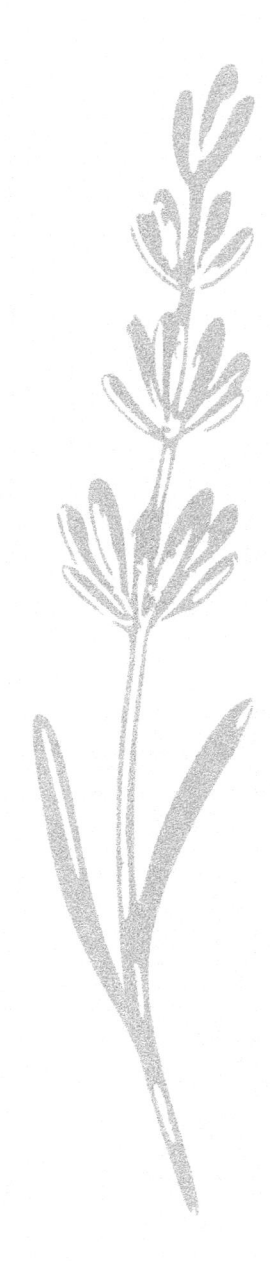

BEFORE THE MATCH

There is always a hush before want—the breath that measures distance.
I keep that silence cupped like a flame not yet declared.
When the spark comes, it isn't lust—it's language.

Every tongue is a torch if you listen closely.

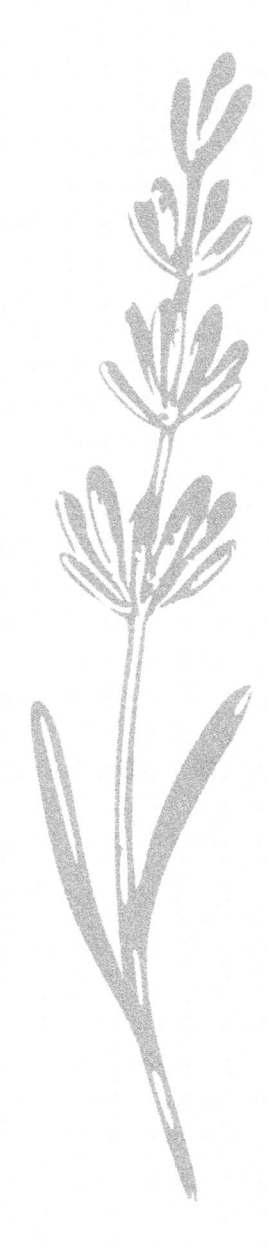

LITANY OF SKIN

Say: I am here.
Say: Touch is translation.
Say: I do not fear being known.

    The body repeats the prayer in muscle and salt.
Sweat is scripture; lips are the ink.
Two mouths make a gospel without shame.

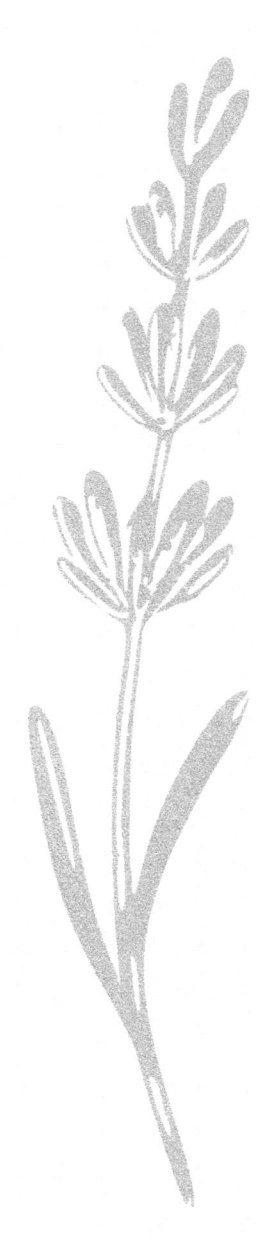

STUDY IN HEAT

Heat doesn't rush—it gathers.
It studies what resists it.
When I lay my hand on another,
I am learning chemistry by heart.

Desire is the experiment that keeps proving tenderness true.

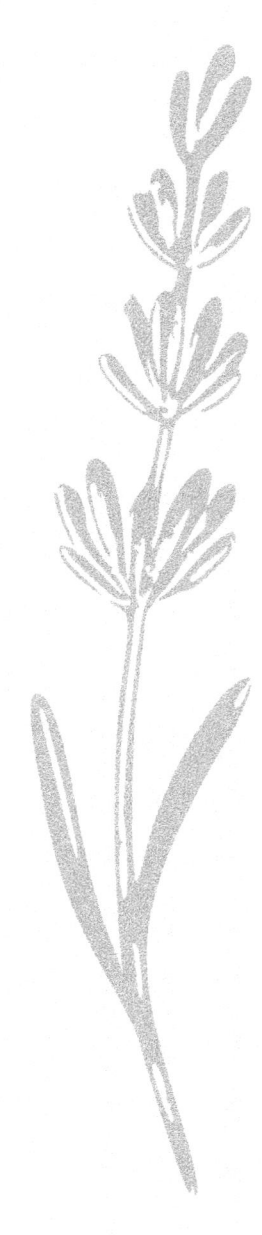

FOR THE BOY WHO FEARED HIS BODY

You hid behind metaphor, called your hips architectural, your chest cathedral ruins.

Now stand here, unadorned.
You are the architecture.
You are the lit candle in the nave.

Let the light reach its own walls.

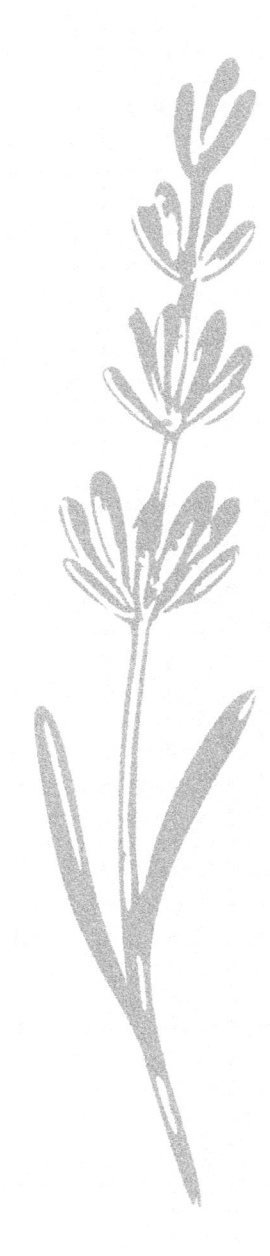

TOUCH THEORY

Every touch is a verb that conjugates mercy.

Past tense: I was afraid.
Present: I am learning.
Future: I will not flinch.

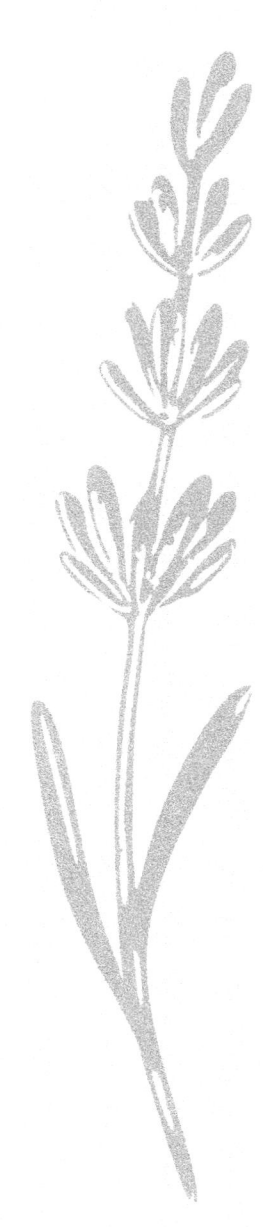

THE CONFESSION OF FIRE

Once I thought flame meant punishment.
Now I know it means remembering warmth.

The match does not apologize for its purpose.
Neither should I.

FIELD NOTE: FRICTION

Observed phenomenon—
Two bodies in proximity create light.
Duration variable; afterglow constant.

Hypothesis confirmed:
Pleasure is proof of life.

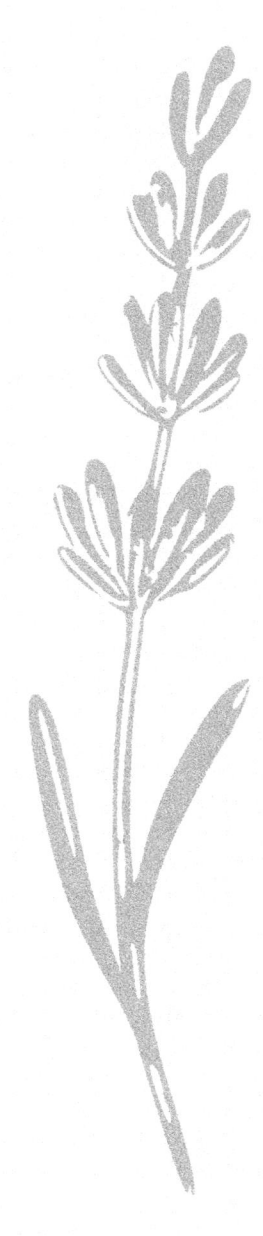

RITUAL OF NAMING

I whispered your name into smoke
and it rose unbroken.
That's how I knew the spell worked.

Every exhale is a letter returned.
Every sigh, a signature.

CANDLE LAB REPORT

Material used: wax, breath, pulse.

Result: room transformed.

Conclusion: illumination requires surrender.

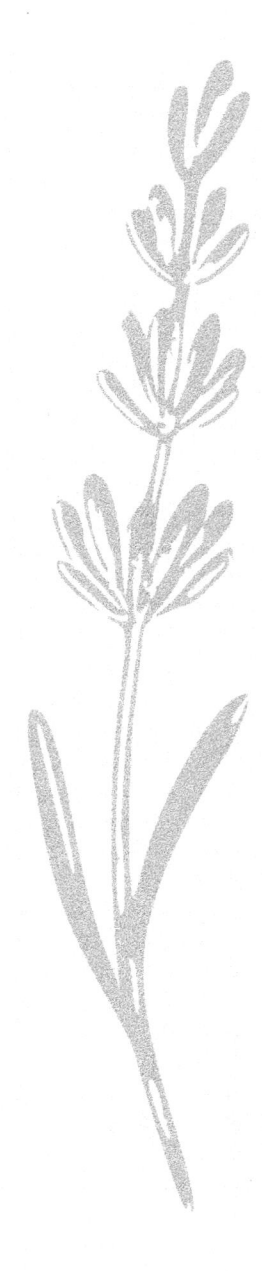

WHEN DESIRE PRAYS

It doesn't kneel.
It stands, eyes open,
hands ready to bless what they've built.

Faith is the body believing in its own spark.

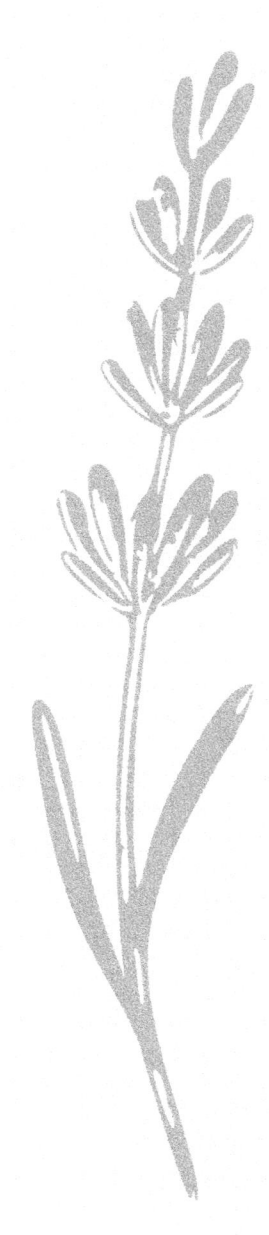

AFTERGLOW AS CARTOGRAPHY

Trace the sweat's path down the spine—
that is how rivers begin.
Mark the freckles; call them towns.
Map the hum between heartbeats; call it nation.

No empire ever held more tenderness than this moment.

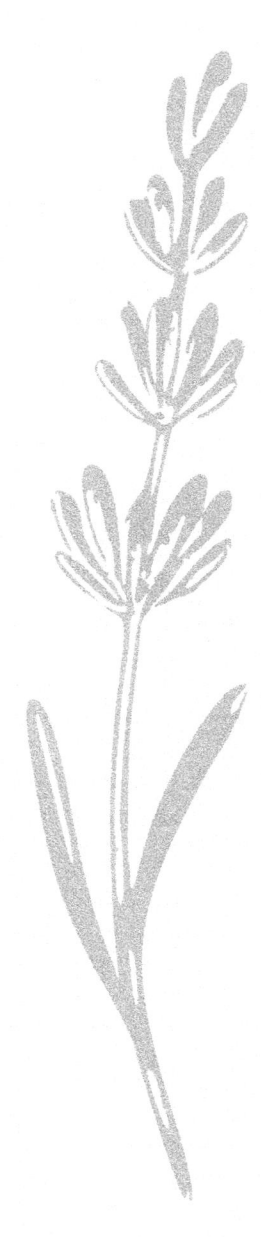

FIELD NOTE: SMOKE

Smoke remembers what the flame forgot.
It carries scent instead of sound.
When I walk through it, I am baptized in echo.

SAGE AND SKIN

I crush sage between my fingers; it releases every room I ever burned in.
The scent climbs the walls, touches the ceiling, returns as permission.

I press my palm to another chest.
Two heartbeats align like struck flints.
Light.

THE LESSON OF ASH

Ash is not an ending.
It is the dust that keeps the shape of what was beautiful.
I draw a circle with it and step inside.
Every spark I ever feared becomes a door.

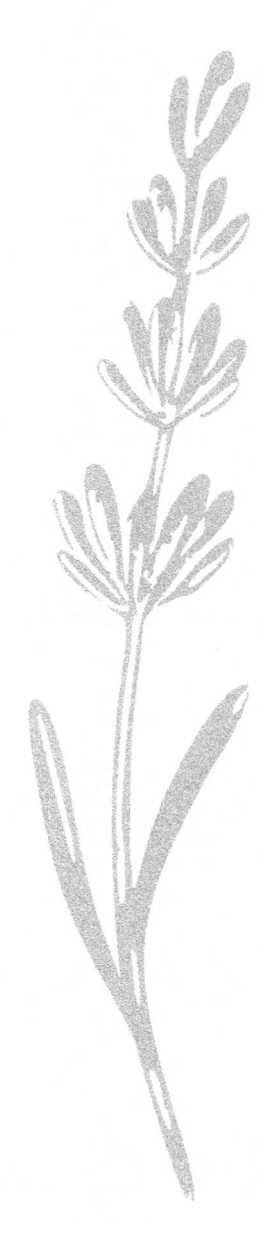

METAMORPHOSIS OF HEAT

Fire → Smoke → Breath → Song.
By the time we finish, the room hums in a key the body invents.

We lie there glowing, and for once the word holy fits.

THE LANTERN TESTAMENT

If I am flame, then you are wick—steadying me.
If you are wax, I am the warmth that gives you shape.
We are our own small constellation of light.

Let no doctrine tell us otherwise.

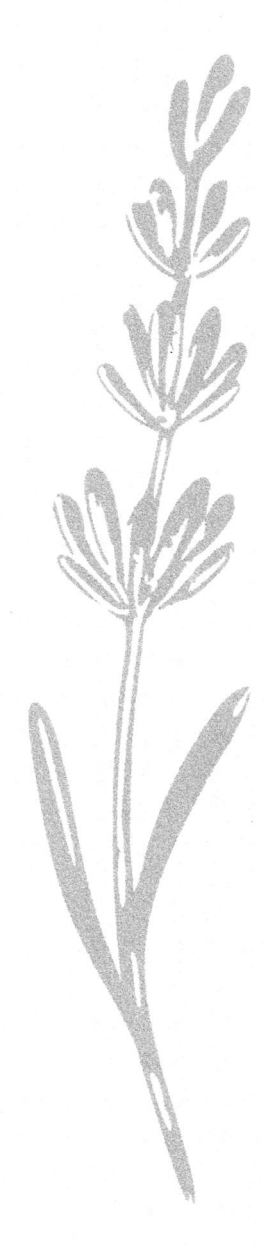

CLOSING INVOCATION — FIRE

THE MATCH BURNS OUT; THE HEAT REMAINS.
SMOKE THREADS THE AIR LIKE HANDWRITING.
I BOW TO WHAT CANNOT BE NAMED WITHOUT TREMBLING.

"From ash, fragrance."

THE ASHES – FIRE RITUAL

△

Stand before the candle. Do not strike the match yet.
Look at your hands — the same hands that touched the earth, the same that were washed clean.

What remains is what burns.

When you light the flame, say the name of what you want to change.
Watch it tremble, then steady.

Desire is not sin; it is alchemy.
Fire asks only that you be honest about what you feed it.

Hold your palm above the flame — close enough to feel the warmth, far enough not to scar.
That space between is where transformation lives.

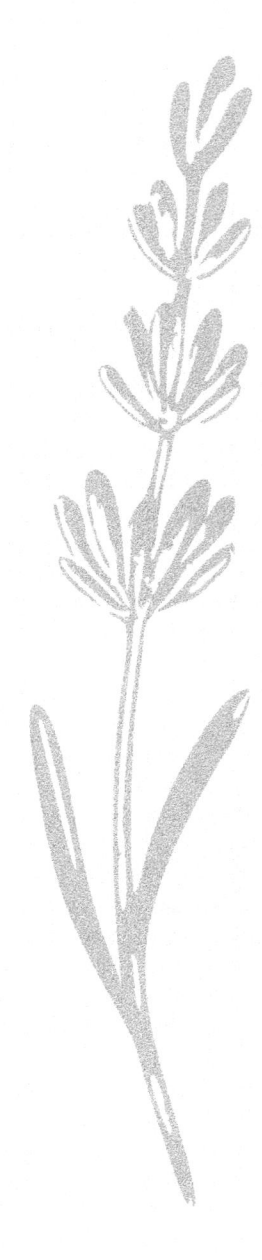

The body is a lantern, the
mouth a prayer.

I burn in the name of
wanting,
and call it holy.

From ash, I learn to touch
again.

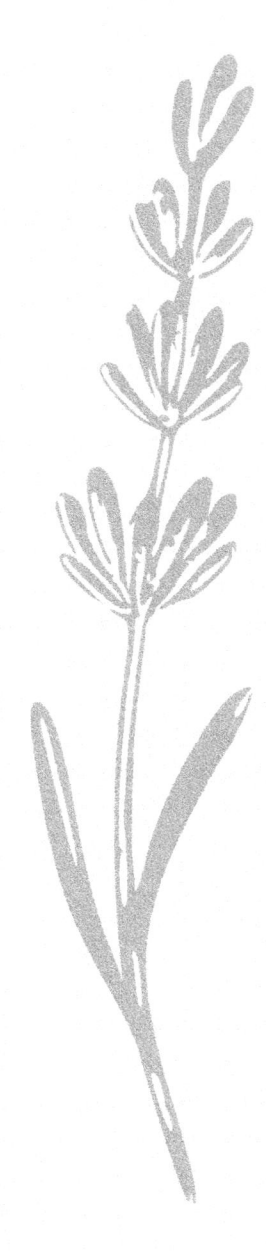

THE DAYS OF CHERRY BLOSSOMS (FORGIVENESS)

THRESHOLD INVOCATION — AIR

"AND STILL, THE SCENT REMAINS."

Open the window. Let the scent move through you.
Speak the name you could not release until now.
The wind will take it—
forgiveness is not forgetting, but flight.

What leaves, returns as light.

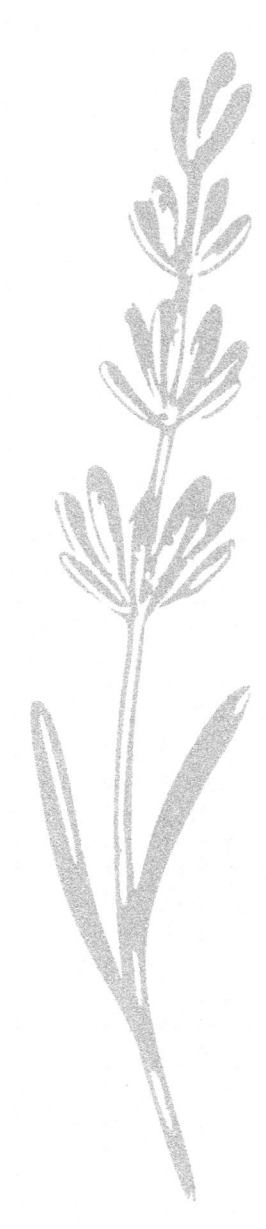

PRELUDE OF PETALS

Morning breaks and the air is already full of memory.
Petals scatter across the porch like torn letters,
each carrying one word: stay, stay, stay.

But the wind is a good teacher—it only holds to let go.
I breathe and feel the house loosen its grip on silence.

This is how seasons speak:
by leaving gently.

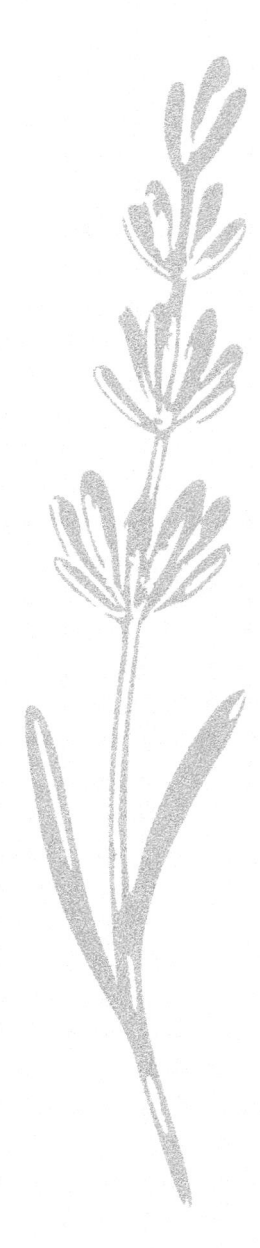

THE WINDOW LESSON

Every pane knows both sides of weather.
You can't choose sunlight without accepting reflection.
I polish the glass until my face fades,
until only the sky answers back.

That, too, is forgiveness—
to stop needing to see yourself in everything.

FIELD NOTE: THE QUIET RETURN

The tree outside the lavender house bloomed overnight.
No thunder, no ceremony—just color.
Forgiveness often arrives that way: unnoticed, absolute.

The roots had their say below ground.
Now the branches whisper it again in pink.

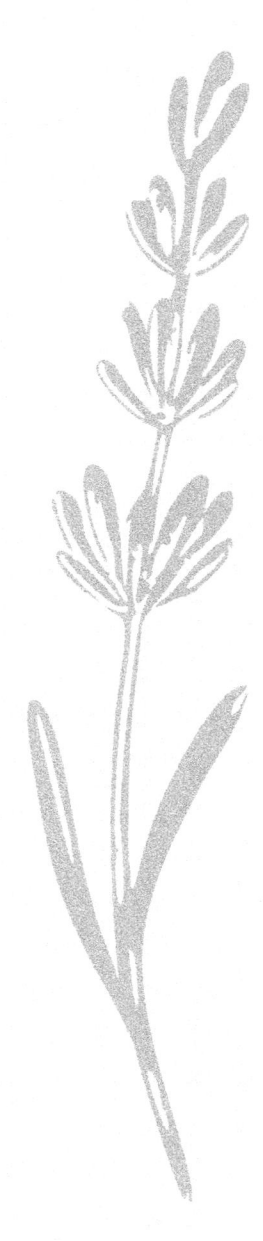

WHAT THE WIND TOLD ME

You can't hold a breeze, it said,
but you can walk with it awhile.
It knows every door you ever closed
and waits patiently for the next one to open.

I asked what comes after healing.
It answered: weather.

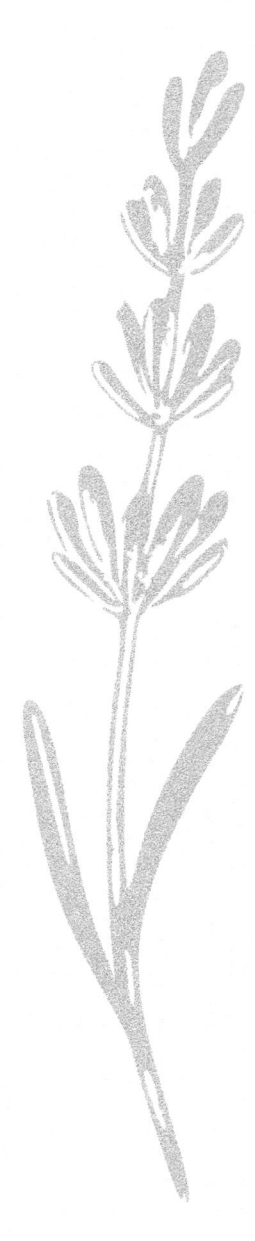

THE WEIGHT OF AIR

Lighter than sorrow, heavier than silence.
It presses just enough to remind you of lungs.

Some days I think the body is made of wind's apprentices—
bones teaching air how to stay a little longer.

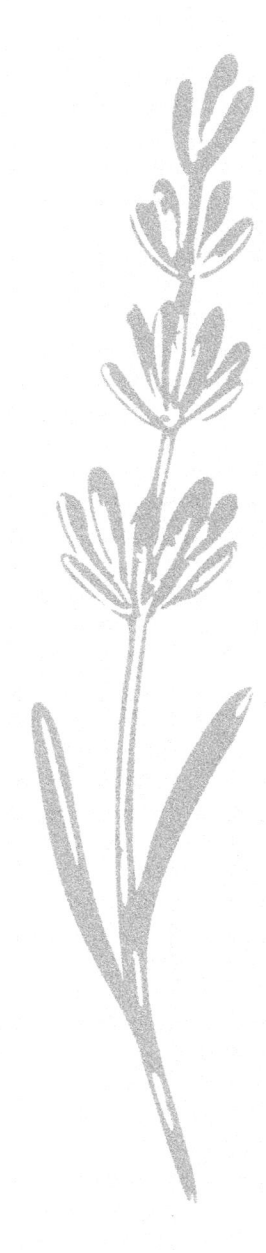

THE BALCONY SCENE

I stepped outside to water the plants.
The city exhaled, and all the noise sounded like relief.
A bus sighed. A bird changed key.
Somewhere a child laughed too loud and didn't apologize.

Forgiveness, I realized, is the world refusing to stay quiet forever.

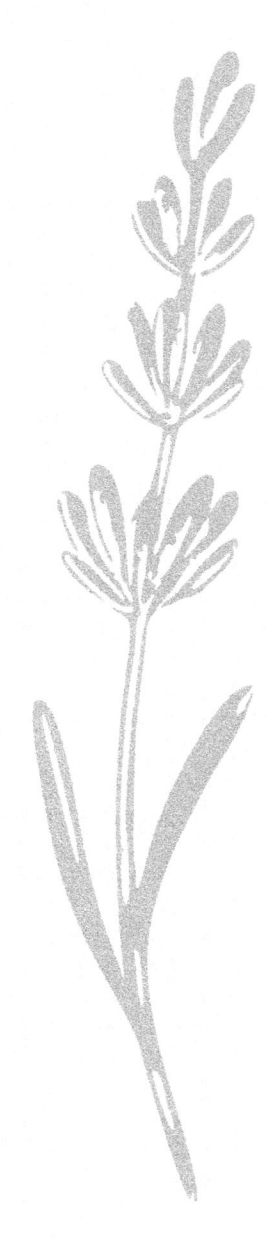

LETTER LEFT UNSENT (FORGIVENESS DRAFT)

Dear you,
I no longer hate the parts of you that stayed when you left.
They've been helping with the dishes.
They remember to feed the cat.

I have stopped trying to burn them out.
They keep the house warmer than I expected.

Yours, still breathing,
WR.

CHERRY-BLOSSOM THEOLOGY

No sermon ever taught me what falling could look like and still be beautiful.
The blossoms did.
They descend together, never ashamed of gravity.
Each petal carries its own small hallelujah.

When I walk through them, I don't pray. I participate.

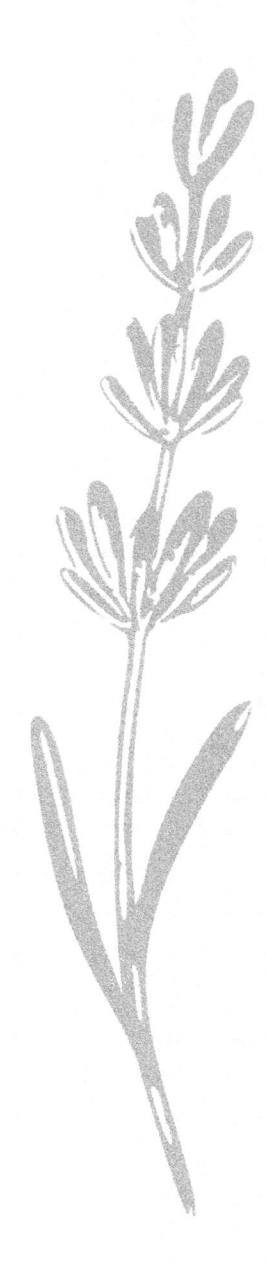

THE LANTERN AT THE WINDOW

The lantern you left on the sill still catches dawn.
Its glass, cracked but serviceable, glows in new grammar:
light through loss, not against it.

I wipe the soot from its edges.
The reflection looks like someone who has learned to stay.

FIELD NOTE: THE RETURN OF THE BEES

After years of quiet, they came back—
circling the lavender in gold arcs of forgiveness.
They do not resent the winter that took them.
They hum, and the garden answers.

Every buzz is a resurrection in lowercase.

THE AIR REMEMBERS

It carries laughter more than names.
It folds old conversations into warmth.
If I stand still long enough,
the breeze moves through me as if I were another open room.

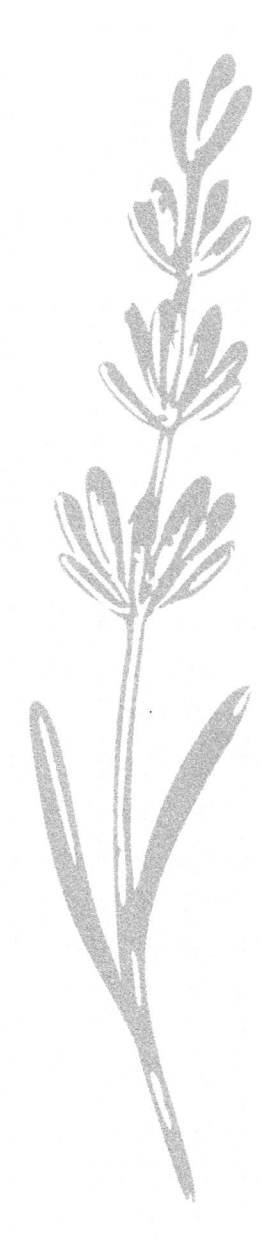

THE NAME OF LIGHT

I whisper yours once more,
not to call you back, but to set you moving.
The sound disperses like dust turning gold.

What remains is brightness.
What remains is me.

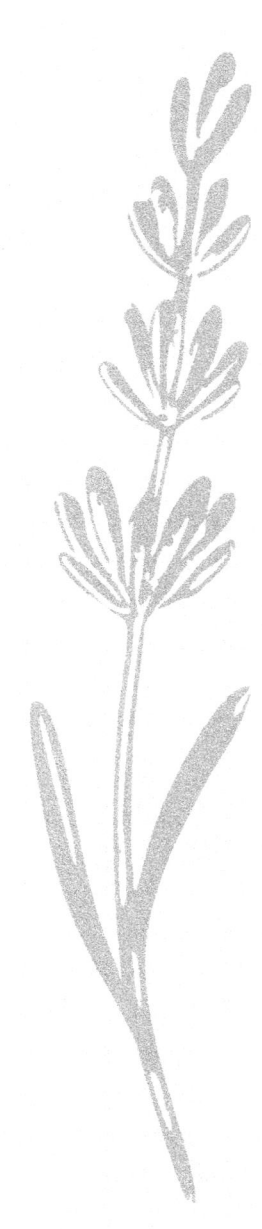

THE LANGUAGE OF LETTING GO

Not all silence is absence.
Some is simply the world inhaling.

I close the window.
The air stays, patient and full of grace.

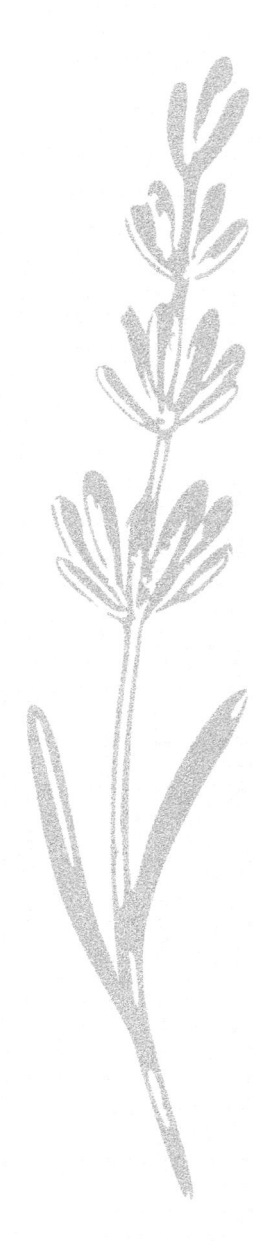

FIELD NOTE: THE HOUSE BREATHES

The boards creak. The curtain sways.
Lavender drifts in again, softer this time.
The air between rooms feels newly washed.

I think the house forgave me first.

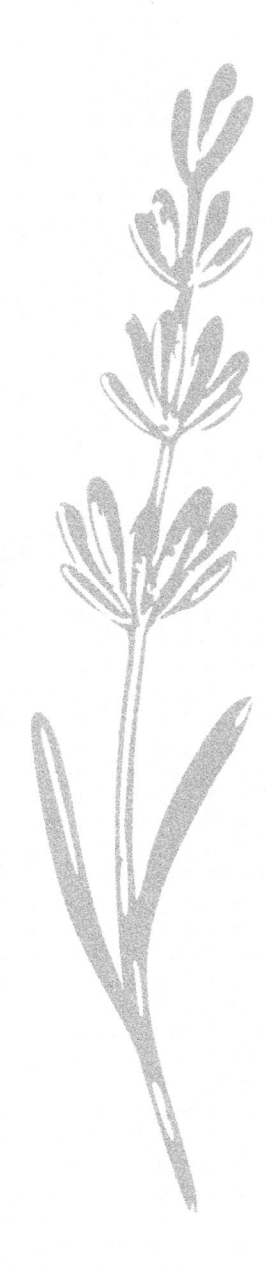

THE ARCHIVIST'S EPILOGUE — FINAL ENTRY

The petals have settled.
The house is still.
Even the ghosts are content to whisper from the rafters.

The boy who buried grief beneath the floorboards has grown into a man who leaves the windows open.

May all readers who enter this house remember: softness is not what survived the fire—it is what made the fire holy.

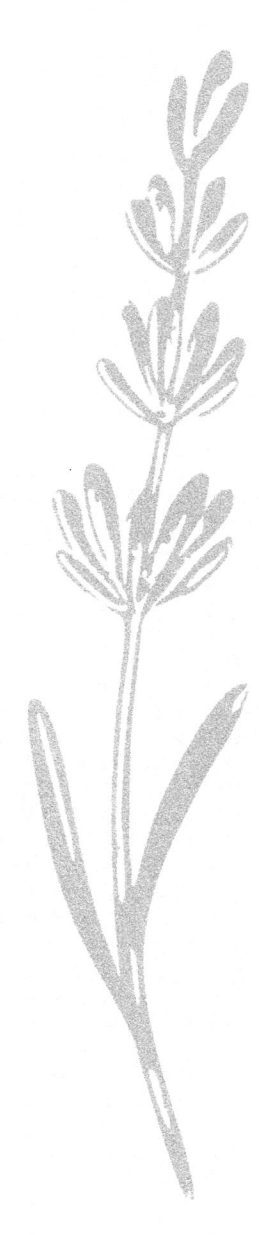

CLOSING INVOCATION — AIR

The wind bows out, carrying names it no longer needs to hold.
I stand in the emptied room,
and the scent that lingers is lavender.

"Forgiveness has wings."

THE DOVE OF MEMORY – AIR RITUAL

△

Open every window. Let the day move through you.
The scent of lavender, of rain, of something unnamed — this is the language of release.

Take a deep breath. Remember one person you have forgiven, and one you haven't.
Speak neither name aloud. The wind already knows them.

Close your eyes. Feel the air moving across your face.
This is how memory breathes — not as burden, but as continuation.

When you open your eyes again, let something go: a folded note, a sigh, a single petal.
Watch it lift and vanish.

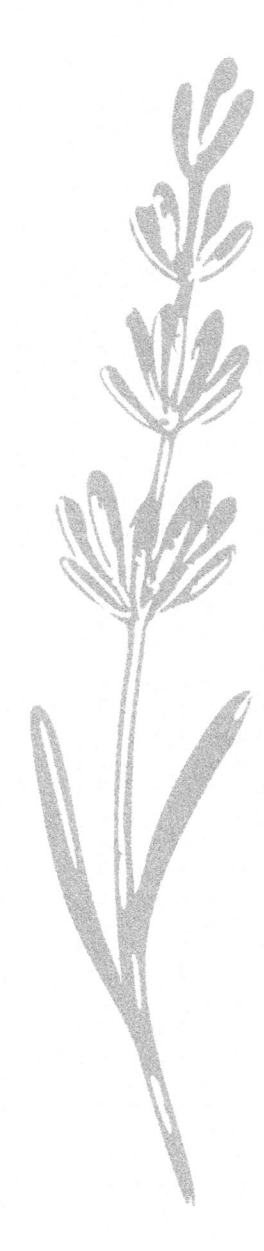

The petals fall like soft confessions.

The wind carries what my tongue cannot.

I breathe, and the world forgives itself.

I follow the scent until it feels like home.

Final Benediction
THE LAVENDER CODEX — CYCLE OF RENEWAL

Each bloom is an element.
Each element, a lesson in staying.

EARTH ▽
The Root Beneath the House

The ground remembers what the heart forgets.

We dug into the silence until it answered.
The roots taught us patience—the first language of resurrection.

WATER ▽
The Embrace

Water does not ask to be held; it asks to hold.

We washed away names until only truth remained.
The reflection was mercy looking back.

FIRE
THE ASHES

From ash, fragrance.

We learned that desire is a kind of prayer,
and every spark is a story choosing light.

AIR
THE DOVE OF MEMORY

Forgiveness has wings.

We opened the window. The scent moved through.
What stayed behind was gentler than silence.

Closing Circle

The soil, the river, the flame, the wind—
all speak the same word: *continue*.

Let the body remember its own seasons.
Let the house breathe.
Let the lavender keep blooming in the cracks.

This is how the story survives—
by scent, by softness, by staying.

Transcribed and sealed by the Archivist beneath the window of the lavender house — Spring, 2025.

Original 2018 Reissue Cover Artwork

The following is the un-edited raw manuscript.

Each page is it's own piece of poetry.

They remain un-named.

Yet are the original seeds planted that bloomed.

Part I:
The Days of Orchids
(Death)

And the taste of whiskey stained your lips
Filling me with a longing of forever.
But we all know forever can never be.
An infinity of lies and broken hearts that should
Show clear,
The trail of bodies we have left.
And the shots that were your eyes,
Made me drown in tides
Of gin and tonic.
Notes of juniper & rosemary
Clouding my judgement
Distilling my inhibitions to bend
At your will.

Oh my love, my heart has been vengeful
And
Tasted jealousy
Because of you.
We drifted apart,
Two worlds colliding in an explosion
Of whiskey and wine.
Our hands can never be cleaned of the blood stains
And teeth marks from the beasts
We have become.
The coffee stains on my hands,
The wine stains in your eyes.
Our stomachs still hanging from our mouths at dawn
As we sobered up and tried to say.
I love you,
One last time.

The feeling of someone else's arms around me
Was immaculate and infinite.
It was like being wrapped in a blanket of lilacs and tulips,
Compared to the moments with you
When it felt like roses,
Whose thorns cut into my delicate flesh.
The taste of your lips
Bourbon still coating them,
Made me intoxicated with a vicious disgust
That I even loved you.

I swam through white lines of cocaine to finally find myself.
Lost.
Alone and truly afraid.
Of falling in love again.
A man so afraid to grow up and learn the ways of being an adult.
I drowned in seas of whiskey to learn it was poison finally.
After so many years of slowly infecting myself with a disease that has no cure, only a temporary relief.
I starved myself for years to keep up this image of self-decay.
Because someone once told me I was self-deprecating, and I needed to grow-up.
I bathed in tides of love.
Always shallow and lacking a depth of what I truly wanted.
A love forever embroidered into the fabric of the universe.
A tapestry piece of true loves greatest disappointment.
That I could ever be loved.
Especially by the likes of someone like you,
Who left me alone for so long and tried to return.
Lover.
Don't come back.

"Towards the future, for it is ours."
You said as we toasted our final goodbyes.
A beautiful moment of loss and learning,
To never fall in love again.
To drown our sorrows
Over cheap wine and hand-rolled cigarettes.
We were saints in disguise of alcoholics.
Saving one another from each other.

Let's go down to church and repent our sins and cleanse our ill spirits of these impoverished thoughts of indulgence.

And by church, I mean to say the nearest bar that we can wash our mouths with cheap booze and lessons of learning to love again once more.

Let's go down to the old oak tree and bind our hands together in a ceremony that will tie us together, forever, as death eats us alive. But the ferryman will never let us pass into the other side, because we have unfinished business.

There may be secrets between us sailors, but sometimes those secrets are better kept together hidden within the sea.

I'm trying to paint you a picture of utter disgust and deceit.

Something to shock & terrify you, something that screams to your name.

A photograph of you in a shoebox locked away for years that I don't need to think about who and what we were. Because we believed love could blossom, and all that grew was death.

And a sense of friendship.

But that's life right, a rat race of emotions that sometimes we can fully understand what is happening. Are so lost in moments of curiosity.

Moments of bliss, appeal, dismay and regrets.

A monolith of emotions erected in your name.

20

Days Of Lavender

A memorial tribute to the days of lavender & sage.

A burial site of loves death.
Yet, I still love you.
And it hurts to say those words.
Yet again.
Let's drink with our weapons exposed.
To show how intent we are on committing a murder.
A death in the family, a small stain of blood.
Forever left to fade over years and remind us of that fateful day.
The day the music died, and lovers ends began.
A somber ritual of mourning will not be held, for no one worth noting would be in attendance.
Soft rains will fall, like tears that drain from dry eyes, a lie of what we had expected to be.

Your eyes led me on a journey searching for blood.
A conquest of spaces.
A determination of finding that shooting star that holds your name in a comets tail.
Lost within glasses of a poison you fed me so graciously and freely.
They held words lacking any substance.
Only giving me a self-defeating pride that I could be better than you.
You laid me down on beds of daggers,
As sharp as your eyes.
That began this journey of bloodlust and yearning.

Like the talons of a peregrine,
You pierced your talons into my flesh
Drawing blood
Eyes wide shut
With a desire to take flight with your kill.
But I merely weighed you down in flight
A heavy burden of baggage
And confused emotions.
I became the artist in the ambulance
Barely holding a poetic heartbeat
Before I flat-lined.
Dead on arrival.

I divulged myself in pills to numb the pains of our break-
up.
I wrote your name in the sands of time,
Hoping that they would finally empty and end my
misery.
I split myself open.
Breaking each rib with rusted tools from the decrepit
shed out back.
Just to see what actually made my heart beat.
I cast spells at midnight to curse ourselves,
Forever under a ritual of never being able to be loved
again.
I slept on railroad tracks,
Waiting for the next train to arrive.
And crush me under its mighty weight.
Splitting me into halves.
As equally broken as I was when you left me.

The glow of your face was like freshly picked bunches of lilacs.
Vibrant and luscious.
But maybe the reason you were shining so brightly like the moon at midnight was because we knew it was over.
A lighthouse in the darkness,
Guiding my way back to you.
An empty home of broken dreams and glorious let-downs with empty promises.

Dead eyes.

Lacking a purpose.

A graveyard of loves risks and tribulations.

A sea of bodies.

Bloated and rotting from decay and improper burial.

My corpse still clings to your headstone.

In hopes that your ghost will follow.

Me into the void.

A child's cry breaks the defining silence of our wasteland.

A single tear spills to the ground.

A sign of the times my love.

"Oh my love.

I've been waiting."

A voice spoke from the darkness.

One so familiar yet so distant.

Lacking purpose.

Lacking empathy.

Lacking love.

Because you never truly loved me.

And I'm sorry for everything.

That glance you gave me from across the bar
Made me laugh just now.
For we will never meet.
Yet our emotionless stares will forever be burned into this forsaken memory of mine.
A steel-trap of my own making.
A labyrinth that even Daedalus & Icarus could never escape from.
But what if I wanted to escape?
From all the excessive baggage that I own.
That I can't seem to store away so finely like everyone else?
How do I become more life you friend?
Lacking so much love and remorse?

You weren't alone in feeling like you were in a bad place.
You just didn't slow down and realized it's a science to falling in love with me.
Because I'm complicated and full of baggage,
Even though I travel lightly.
I'm a wanderer.
A loner.
A self-decaying mold of a pretentious form of what I should act like,
Because I am "that kind of person."
Did you ever realize how much your words cut like knives?
How they pierced my flesh a thousand times,
Over and over,
Bleeding me dry of any color of life.
Did you realize how much you had damaged me,
Even after the fact?
Curious minds are full of wonder and piqued interest.
I still carry your photo in my wallet
And I can never tell you the truth about why.
Because of our sordid affair.

I still have feelings for you,
Even after we have been away for so long.
Every end has a beginning
With pointed fins in the shape of teeth
Barred to bite.
To suck blood from each other's open wounds
And deliver it back pure and clean.
To breath the universe,
In
And
Out.
Fueling a kaleidoscope of sin and sex into some form of romantic
Bullshit.

You looked so surprised to see me again that day.
As if though nothing had ever happened.
That a tear in the fabric of the universe had never happened.
As though,
You had never fallen in love before.
With someone so full of it,
That it bled from my skin.
And in the kisses that I gave to you.
Delivered twice over with such force and compassion.
Did you know that every kiss is different?
A sad disappointment of what could and couldn't ever be.
Every glance I give,
Every careless lie,
Every somber lull of sighs.
Rolling from my lungs.
Growing like orchids from my chest,
Breathing and dying each time.
A symbol of hope and defeat.

You praised me like God.
Drank my blood like wine
And ate my flesh
Like communal bread.
Hoping I could be your savior.

There's so much lost love in the atmosphere.
And some parts of it are flooding into me,
Even though I don't want to be loved again.
I'm afraid and in love
Yet at the same time ashamed to admit I want to be loved.
Time is the illusion and instigator now,
Time is the one fucking everything up.
Or maybe it's the bourbon talking.
Maybe it's the universe screaming your name,
Telling me to tear away
Yet at the same time stay.
"But oh my love, how I've missed you."
Missed you.
Calling your name into the atmosphere.
Screaming for a change I'm afraid I can't escape because
I'm afraid to
Break another heart.
Although now I have to wonder,
How many have I broken before without ever thinking
about it?
Has it always been me,
Or you?
Oh my love,
How I've missed you.
That night still haunts my dreams.
The night I realized the truth.
The truth of you & I.
That we are no longer.
And it's all because you have me wrapped
Around your finger.

Encompass the black sea
Beneath my eyes
A love so
Far lost
And dead
Can you see
What I see?

And you drank from my mouth
A poison so delicate
That you've never tasted before.
Something intoxicating and painful
At the same time
Because I have such sights to show you my love.
Vast wastelands of nothingness,
Loneliness and despair.
Killed over years of self-defeat
And an unwillingness
To accept.
Barren trees
Slivers of birch and elm
Clutching outward
As if to hold you
Once more
And feel
An
Embrace of
Skin.

Do these words make you nervous?
They should.
Do they hold your history?
They do.
Do they have the power to control you?
Only if you believe it my love.
Do you know how I made you fall?
With only one kiss.
Do you know how I don't love you anymore?
Because I close my eyes.

Sometimes I contemplate
If it's just me
Or you?
In how much I ponder
Who I am
As a person of this
Society.
Do you know me.
Do I know you.
Have we fucked.
Have we kissed.
Have we experienced a moment together.
Or is it me
Just wondering
How much you immersed me
Into the value
Of being
This person.

We rode into the galaxy ablaze

On the coat-tails of a comet

Searching the asteroid belts

For some sign of life

And love.

But space is a lonely place

For us astronauts.

An infinity of expanse

With no direction

And no forgiveness.

We mined planets for love

Only finding they were dead

And have been for such a long time.

Just like our love

Alone in the coldest of places.

Never to feel an intimate embrace

Of skin

And warmth

From another celestial body

Like yours.

The cards spoke a truth of second comings.
A rebirth from the dead past that once was us.
Shouting into the ether that good things were on the horizon.
New and prospective tidings of creative expression and a release of unused second-rate feelings.
A reprieve from the rough losses that have befallen me, a sign of the times.
They spoke in symbols of Knights & Pentacles, a sacred geometry linked to the cosmos.
Ideals of prosperity and my cup overflowing into a torrential river.
To stop this love drought.

Did you fall into me like I fell into you?
Failing to keep our guards up.
With swords dangling carelessly above us.
Did you hear their voices sing in unison when I kissed you?
Pushing you against the wall with such passion of fever and desire.
Did you realize the moment I stopped caring was earlier that we cared to stop learning?
Because it's clear we were never meant to be.

The stars aligned in new constellations when we met.
Disavowing from the laws of nature to shout from caves and shores far off.
Echoing through space & time.
To travel back to you.
Hoping the message was clear.
I don't love you.

As I viciously smoked what I believed to be my last cigarette,
Like the time I said I was over you,
I couldn't help but feel a sense of pride wash over me.
Something so lost in myself I forgot that I ever even had it.
I once was full of confidence.
I smiled. Everyday. I laughed. At every silly joke.
Then you broke my heart.
And each cigarette was a pact with the devil that I wanted to die quicker so I could forget the past.
And break your fucking heart for once

For I am the king of this pity party with my jewel encrusted crown and a single tear that is forever stained upon my cheek from the day that I learned to stop expecting all of the world around me to love and be loved.

A proclamation to the last moments of a dying history based on drunken laments and drug fueled lucid dreams of grandeur.

A lesson imprinted on the palm of my hands, like the peaks and valleys that cause the way lines on the map that I created.

In hopeful attempts that you would find your way back home to me someday soon.

You gave me bouquets of orchids and sunflowers to declare your love and hate for me at the same time.
Signs of a new beginning.
Symbols of a death so inevitable.
A history already dismounted from text books.
A future dislodged from the universal timeline.
Written on your hands.
Follow the heart lines.
Stray from the lifelines.
Traverse the twisting fates of your element.
Become lost once more in the ever-changing ebb & flow of what could have been You & I.

Stark naked and alone in a world so cold & despite.
Devoid of any romance.
Any chance of luck & new beginnings.
But there's a glimmer of hope my young cardinal.
A beacon of hope.
Shimmering in the void of this selfless dominance of life.
A single arrow shot into the air, glowing with wisps of blood-orange kisses.
Lapping at the fringe of the darkness.
Craving the turn of a book to the next page.
To tell the tale of a better tomorrow.
To show the victory of the final showdown between the devil & god.
Who are raging inside of me.

Hypnotic moves.
Is the only way I can describe how your hips swayed.
Captivating my tired eyes.
With each thrust you gave.
Driving your love & passion.
Deeper inside of my soul.
An ecstatic ritual of lust & desire.
For carnal indulgences.
Your hands searching the secret passageways.
Of my heart.
Navigating the ever-changing complexity.
Of my labyrinth I created.
Just to keep you out.
Yet a navigator of the soul, you found a way.
To see the truth from fiction in the paranoid abyss.
That is my heart.

Self-righteousness looks so perfect on you my love.
Such vanity and lack of emotions.
I strive for those days of ignorant bliss, but altogether don't crave ever being a part of your sense of well-being.
You can wave your flag proud.
But you're still a coward in sheep's clothes that cries at night.
You wet the bed when you have a nightmare.
Can you run your mouth as lovely as you swing your hips my dear?
To preach to a choir in which no one cares to actually hear?
Do you truly believe you are deserving of sharing the same space as me?
The sign read like this:

WE
CAME
HERE
TO GET
AWAY
FROM
YOU.

Original Artwork/Inspiration

© John Criscitello

The devil and god are raging inside of me
A clash of titans
A war that has waged since before even my time.
A battle to the death of who and what I am,
And where it will leave the end result
Of
I & I.

It's like watching moths flock to a flame
An elegant ball of impending destruction of the soul.
To see them carelessly & feverously throw so much caution
Into the wind.
With no care for a safety net or a guidance of purpose.
Just the self-realization that they are better than themselves.
For this is the Lord's day, and Jesus didn't take the wheel.
The devil did.
He's a speed demon with a bad coke habit
Driving at 170 MPH all the way home
With me by his side
Like Bonnie & Clyde.
Lost cares & concerns thrown into the wind.

To even think that you would be
interested in ME as more than
just another fucking lay.
What a joking matter.
A sense of pride overcame me
knowing that just because I dressed
so cute.
I managed to catch your eye.

Part II:
The Days of Lavender
(Rebirth)

The ocean wept tears of joy
When you kissed me in the dusk hours
On that park bench you took me to.
The birds sang a chorus of hymns and burning desire
In hopes that you really were real.
The skies didn't break open and rain down love
But my mouth parted and spoke words.
"I just want to kiss you."
"I'd like that very much."
Don't get caught stealing kisses in the night
Or you'll end up like me.
A thief of hearts.
A hopeless drunken romantic
Falling at the first touch & kiss I experience.

And like a flame in the darkness dying
From a lack of oxygen
The night came.
Just like me
After you touched & kissed me
Softly
As you cradled my head
In your hands.

My words are the most vulgar and desperate plea
Of a love never given.
A void in my chest
In the shape of you.
A place I want to call
Home.
Filled with a love that is grown
Not gifted
I'm terrified of losing that feeling
Once again.
That feeling of letting go
Of my fear and inhibitions.
A loss that drains into
The decaying watersheds
Of the cosmos.

I want to return to the Days of Lavender.
A place where the scent of lilacs and orchids
Bloomed so freely when we walked through
The darkness together to view
The ever-changing tides
Of the universe.
You, slowly slipping your hand into mine.
Did you mean to do that,
Or did I make you?
I can't recall.
The Days of Lavender,
Where the sun beamed down on you as we ate dinner
And confessed our earliest memories and traumas
To each other.
Voicing how vulnerable we are to one another.
The Days of Lavender.
Where you asked me out for ice cream
On a Monday.
Because when I'm with you
It smells like home.
And it makes me smile once again.
Oh those beautiful,
Days of Lavender.

It's been a year now.
That was the last time I truly thought about you.
A fleeting glance of a memory untold to anyone.
Something that felt like a dream,
Yet altogether a nightmare.
Locked away in the recesses of my mind.
A place that never knew
Who you were or the fact you existed.
Like looking in a mirror and seeing only myself.
It's been only twenty minutes.
Since I last thought of and met
Someone who's scent devoured me
Like yours.

I'm sorry that I managed to catch you at my worst.
Telling you.
Show me,
Show me,
Show me,
How you do that trick.
But honestly, how do you do that trick?
With a passion that you showed me,
Engulfing my body in flames.
Burning my soul on overdrive,
Craving your touch & kiss.

I waited a thousand days for the chance to see you again.
I blood-let myself into vases to make roses bloom
So I could pluck one for each day I had to wait.
What grew wasn't flowers.
It was something more incredible.
A heart.
One filled with years of wisdom and cunning charm
That would one day soon,
Be gifted to you.
The most sacred exchange of priceless gold.
Something to give purpose and drive.
To lose is to gain.
To learn to let go of it all.

We traversed through landscapes of new adventures.
Through the glades of evergreens and Douglas firs
Becoming ever more lost in ourselves.
Through the long nights and endless sunsets
That were ahead of us.
I desired nothing more than to revel,
In one more kiss with you.
To feel one more passionate excitement.
To drive pride and confidence
Into my being.
Alive with the universe,
Breathing each loss through one another.
Locking hands in an ecstatic dance
Of joy and perpetual indulgences.

What makes you excited my dear?
What inner workings of cogs and gears turns
To make you tick?
Who are the monsters under your bed
That keep you up at night?
Where are those golden gods you praised
for hoping of a savior
To save you from these impending dismal tragedies
Looming on the horizon.
When are the tides of change
To break their course of action
And break free from the traditions
Of Us?
Why are you so pensive
To let me open the door
And let the demons eat away
At our imperfections?

The sweetest of meats is the fear instilled in all of us.
The fear of rejection.
The fear of being less than.
The fear of being young at heart.
The bitterest of herbs,
Poured into our open wounds felt like salt.
A symbol of never letting the past die.
You left a taste so bittersweet in my mouth
That I had to wonder.
Why you would poison the well from which we both drink from?
To infect the populace of the world with the Word of Love.
A thing so infectious & deadly that even years later I still haven't found a cure.

Sleep in eternal slumber my love
For that is where we will always find each other.
In daydreams and nightmares.
Created by Morpheus.
Spread the sand across my cursed body
If you ever feel like seeing me again
Once more.

Broken and dead languages are what we spoke in.
Hoping that our rusty translations were enough
To capture the value of me telling you
I like you.
I never learned how to speak French
But mon cherie
I can woo you with my charm and intellect
Unlike these other boys.
A language of our own creation
That we as poets can only understand.
The languhge of love.
A thing built on self-righteous confidence and demoralizing pride
That we are better than those around us.

There was the sound of wedding bells
That chimed in the distance as you walked away
For the final time.
Were they meant for us
Or for the lost souls who found a self-fabricated love
To divulge for years of denial
That you never loved them?
Or where they meant for us?
A question of both our faiths and dedication to be
Powerful
&
Infinite.
Did it hurt when you said those words to me that fateful day?
Was it because I missed your birthday?
I'm sorry I'm self-absorbed and a worthless sack of flesh,
Driving a body of meat,
But I'm only human like you are.

The peaks of mountains are cold and lacking life, like the way that I wake up each morning to an empty bed.
I stir to find you, hoping that it was all a bad dream that we had to let go.
But sometimes we have to move forward to let go of the past right? What if I can't let go of the past because I like being haunted.
Haunted by the family of ghosts that I never learned to love back.
The spirits of everyone I never loved.
I wake each morning desperate only gaining a sense of closure when I cry in the shower.

When I die
I want you to lay
Sunflowers on my grave.
Where it will mark
A symbol of hope,
That I finally can feel the sunshine
Once more.
Don't weep over my coffin as
It is empty and my corpse
Is elsewhere.
Let one balloon fly into the sky
And tie a ribbon of gold around it
So that when it reaches me in Heaven
I can know that you loved me.

How long did it take you to muster the courage
To want to reach out to me.
To touch me
In the darkness.
To bleed light into such a bleak space.
How long did it take you to gain your pride
To want to sweep me off my feet.
To lift me up high
Into the sky.
To make me fly.
How long did it take you to plan your speech
To tell me one final time
I don't love you.
In such eloquence and unavailable
Dismay.
How long did it take you to find your next fix
To take the hand of another
And tell them I love you.

We never did go for ice cream that fateful Monday.
And it broke my heart.
But the message you text was heart-warming and sincere.
"I fear that I've been single so long that I've put up some walls/barriers. I need to do more personal work before putting myself back out there."
And I understand, because I'm going through the same exact thing my love.
At least there's always the chance of catching up over a beer along the journey, with a soul that cares for you.

I was taught for so many years to hate myself
And deny every moment and memory of who I am.
I was taught that silence was a golden virtue
A value of speaking when spoken to.
But now that I've grown up
I've learned to speak with brevity
And confidence.
Walking tall and proud on my best days
And something short of wearing a mask on others.
Something I'm working on still,
Thanks to you.

How many times can we die
To learn
That fate has
A funny way
Of placing us
In the right place
At the right time.
Sometimes with the completely wrong person.

How long until the drugs begin to take us on this journey of love?
How long until the morphine kicks in an numbs us to the pains of what will soon be inevitable?
How long until the penicillin starts to work to cleanse our open wounds, we so carelessly inflicted on each other out of spite and regrets?
How long until the medical salves Indian witch doctors gave us, brings us back into a surreal idea of falling in love all over again.
How long until the tea leaves begin to read us the truths of our future and past?
How long until the clay masks we placed on our faces crack & dry, beginning to expose all the fissures and infected parts of ourselves?
How long until we are baptized in the waters of the universe, drowning one another a thousand times to save each other from our present.

I'm floating a thousand feet from the ground
Because you made my head feel like a balloon.
And I know I'll fall,
Crashing head first into the foothills of jagged rock faces and snow-capped romances.
I awoke to find myself cold and caught in a blizzard of words.
Biting my cheek ever so lightly, like the times you would bite my neck so gently and passionately.
Wrapping itself around me, devouring, with a vicious intent to smother me.
"Would you like to come in out of the storm?" You asked, as your hand pulled me through the door.
And you softly placed me on the bed.
Stripped me of my youth and took my virginity.
"Never let me go."
Is all I asked of you.

Summer vibes and hot guys is the all-American wet dream. Drinking cocktails on patio bars, laughing as we slowly burn ourselves alive.
Although all I want to do is be right next to you, holding your hand. Looking deeper and deeper into the oceans that are your eyes, drowning in cascades of sorrow & floating in ebb tides of remorse.
I want to be under the blankets, hidden from society, but not you.
If we must go out, can we at least stay in the shade, where I can hide my pale flesh from becoming the color of rose-tinted glasses.
I personally prefer green-tinted, but red seems more fitting for the times you instilled a fiery yearning into my body.
Because jealousy never suited my taste.

"I'm sorry it took me forever to get home. My flight was delayed!"
Was the last thing I ever heard from you that night.
The night the ballad of love & hate sang clearly across my universe.
The night you were taken from me.
"It's fine. I'll see you when you get home. I can't wait to kiss you mister. I love you."
Was the last thing I ever sent to you.
The night I was taken from you.

I stood over myself in those final moments. Staring at the image of decay and desperate pity that was my lifeless body. Drowning in a pool of blood and bath-water so impure and unclean, like my soul. I never knew that I looked so unwanted before until this moment. I noticed every detail of what I hated the most. The slight cow-lick on my forehead, the forever blackened bags under my eyes. The lanky skeleton of my emaciated body crumpled on the bathroom floor. I didn't even notice when you walked in and ran to me, spilling a thousand tears that mixed into a vivid mixture of morbid art. If only I could take back that moment and return back to you my love, but who could ever love a family of ghosts like you did?

I'VE TASTED DEFEAT AND NOW I WANT REVENGE.

I PICKED UP A PEN AS A SIGN OF JUSTICE, TO PROVE THAT I CAN CREATE SOMETHING SO POWERFUL AND MAGNIFICENT. BUT AT THE SAME TIME DAMAGE AND DESTROY YOU WITHOUT EVER SAYING A WORD.

I'VE TASTED BLOOD AND NOW I WANT WINE.

THE TASTE BECOME THICK AND VISCOUS, SOILING MY TONGUE WITH THE TASTE OF ACRID METALS AND SPOILED SINS.

I'VE DIVULGED MYSELF INTO CARNAL PASSIONS.

TIE ME UP, UNTIE ME.

I'VE CREATED A NEW RELIGION.

AND CALLED MYSELF A GOD

TO DISHONOR YOU.

OUR FATHER. (WHO ART IN HEAVEN.)

My head was spinning
Full of acid
Staring at the sand-dunes
Forming in the bed sheets.
I searched for miles through the desert,
In hopes to find you.
But you were just a mirage.

I hate myself because of you.

I drowned in all of the poison you were last night, and it left me broken and bruised in the morning.

I tried everything to just feel a little closer to you because I can't be a human.

I let you go and came running back to your open arms.

I was afraid of missing something.

When I awoke, I realized I didn't need you.

Because you made me addicted.

Can we dance under the starlight, the cosmic vibrancy of our exposed skin touching ever so gently?
We must not disturb the universe because it's oh so quiet right now.
Can we play our favorite songs and gaze into the constellations, pondering the true value of what we could be?
We have to walk softly with our bare feet exposed as to not disturb the earth,
For She is alive and breathing.
Can we kiss a thousand times over, sealing our moments of lust into envelopes and send them to each other?
We have to hold on tight, as the ocean is becoming violent.
Can we build a makeshift boat out of sticks and hope and sail through our dreams once again?
We have to drink careful and steadily, as our weapons have not been exposed yet.
Can we rediscover ourselves in these moments?
For the door is waiting to be opened, and She is asking us to come inside.

I'm burning up inside and it hurts.
Everything hurts.
My body aches, my throat is dry, my forehead beading with sweat.
I'm burning up and I have no control.
I'm feverish and about to have an anxiety attack.
I'm feverish and I feel uncomfortable.
I'm fevering and I'm afraid of what is happening.
I'm feverish and I just want to be comforted.
I'm feverish and I don't know what to do.
When you're not around.

I can only fit so many words
Into one text.
Before they start bleeding
Out of my mouth and onto paper.
I can only say so much to you
In person when I'm not sober.
I'm a profound mess,
And I just want you.
To be my Saint.

Cotton candy flavored wet-dreams made
of cherry waves
is what I imagined my first kiss
with you would taste like.
To be devoured by your scent
becoming entangled in memories
of what used to be a home
I once believed in.
Drunk off of lapping
at the seas of pink lemonade
where you threw my words in
perfectly tucked away
in glass bottles.
You fed me blood-oranges and strawberries
coated in lust & desire
slowly placing candies
across my naked torso.
To slowly kiss them
from the freckles
where you destined them to live.
The taste of absinthe
still coating your lips
is all that I can ever recall
from that dream though.
You still can eat me alive if you wanted to boy.
To place your lips on sacred temples
kiss the feet of gods.
To leave your gifts tucked away
in the nooks and cracks of my damaged soul.
You can still kiss me.
Whenever you want.

Part III:
The Days of Sage
(Sex)

"Will you fuck me like you do all the other boys you've had in your bed?"

"Fuck me and leave."

That's all I ask for. I don't want your emotions or baggage. I just want the desire inside your pants. I want to praise my own god, and not you.

"That's right, I want you to cum in me."

Right where I have you, caught between the cross-hairs of the hunter's rifle.

I want to take your essence and keep it forever.

"Fuck. I'm going to cum."

"I love you."

"I love you too."

I didn't kick you out of bed when I should have.

The people next door must hate me
for how loud I have sex with guys like you.
Or maybe for the many nights I've had to jerk off alone
because I'm such a shallow and shy man.
Or maybe it's the endless clacking of the keys of my
typewriter
when I pen these hopeless words full of vibrancies and
stunning visuals to paint these pictures that belong in
museums.
I think it's maybe because of how rough I toss you
around the room, falling into forward and never letting
go.
Because sometimes I just want to put your head through
the wall, and others I want to hold you close to me and
never let you go.

Your pink cellphone,
Buzzed through the airways of the world,
Electrifying and pulsing
White lies to every corner of the globe.
Your pink cellphone,
The one with all the evidence of our homicide.
Your pink cellphone.
That I always look at and wonder why you left.
Your pink cellphone.
Faded on emptiness and a lack of memory
Because I can't delete your photos from it just yet.

Tie me up.
Untie me.
Place the gag in my mouth and tell me I'm your slave.
There's a song for that, you should look it up.
But I'm no one's slave, only a master of my own.
I may want to suck the desire out of you,
And feed upon your lips a thousand times
Like a babe craving its mothers' tit for more milk,
But all I truly crave is the intimacy of your touch.

The way your hands clutched at my throat
Just short of choking me,
Just enough to turn me on,
Kept me enthralled by you.
Dominating,
Commanding,
Coded and methodical.
I experienced new sensations,
I buried my heads in the sand
While you ate away my ass.
You pushed yourself into me
With such a vigor and anger
I had to cry out.
Don't make it hurt anymore,
Daddy.
I'm not your little boy any longer
And I have needs to be satisfied
Just like you do.
So fuck me like the little whore
You want me to be
And hold me close afterwards.
Whispering to me
The sweetest of nothings.
And craft my dreams into
The stars you talked about
That you see in my eyes.

Fuck me in the shower,
Fuck me in the woods,
Fuck me in the bathroom at work
While I'm on break,
I'm yours for the taking
And I've my fruit is just ripe enough
For your tongue to taste
And devour.
To suck,
And lick
And savor.
The sweet delicacy of such a pure
And innocent young man.
To make the roses bleed.
"Don't worry about the blood stains, it'll be alright."
You said.
But it never was.
I never could feel whole again after that night.

Have you tasted my fruits,
The ones that She birthed me with,
Awaiting your call.
To deliver them to you.
For your spirit to devour and feast upon
Because I starved you
For so long.
She has come
&
So have I.

I HAVE THIS FANTASY OF TYING YOU UP,
IN THE WOODS.
LEFT ALONE, WAITING, NOT KNOWING IF I'LL EVER COME BACK.
JUST YOU.
NAKED.
BOUND TO A TREE.
SO I CAN COME BACK TO YOU
AND RELEASE MYSELF INSIDE THE WILDEST OF ANIMALS.

How long
Have your eyes
Undressed me
In ways that
Even the
Devil would blush?
How long
Has your mouth
Been craving the
Taste of my flesh
Supple and tender?
How long
Have you been
Hard in your groin
Imagining every second
Of slowly entering
My soul?
How long
Have you
Wondered what it felt like
To fuck someone
So emotional
And depressed.
How long Did it take you
To stop laughing at me
For crying when
Slept together?
How much
Did you manage
To destroy of my Soul
Before you came?

You asked me what I was into:
I told you I was open-minded.
You slipped something strong into my drink:
I told you I didn't want that.
You threw me onto the bed:
I couldn't move.
You bound me to the bedpost:
I was helpless.
You took a piece of me:
And I couldn't do anything.
You came all over my face:
I was forced to drink your poison.
You slapped me:
A disgraceful shame that I couldn't be better.

The way your hands moved with such eloquence across my face, like a sculptor studying his canvas, plotting the points to drive his chisel and hammer into.
To create the defining lines of his greatest masterpiece, you did exactly the same with me.
Rough hands, studying each curve and contour of my face. Slowly following my neckline downwards.
Slithering across my chest, ink stains and freckles guiding your ever-searching tongue for a place to rest.
You rested upon my stomach, kissing and craving each quiver I returned back to you.
Hands twisting around me, grasping me closer, as your mouth found the inner parts of my thighs. (The most delicate of places on a man they say)
You threw my legs around your shoulders, staring intently at me the entire time. Your eyes bright and burning full of a fiery desire to devour me.
You split me open and gave me the blood of reptiles. Delivered twice over in one moment,
To show how much we were bound to be together.

Did you see god
When I made you cum?
Or did you
Finally just learn
What an orgasm
Actually felt like?

Sexuality was always taboo in my family
a thing never spoken about but known.
"The Gay One"
The boy who was so different.
I knew that I had a sexual appetite for men when I was 9.
I can recall everything about him.
His name. His scent. His body.
The boy next door. The one who made me get down on
my knees and blow him in the banquet hall behind his
father's bar. Because that's what good boys do, right?
He smelled like lilacs and freshly plucked daisies with a
hint of musk.
He was the All-American Dream Boy.
The first time we fucked was on his father's waterbed.
The waves thrusting him further and further inside me,
even though we never knew what lube was.
We fooled around for a few months, until one day we got
caught.
His cum still dripping down my face after he spewed his
load all over it.
He moved away, and I never saw him again.
But I still smell him on the breeze and search for him
when that old familiar aroma greets hello.

Part IV:
Days of Cherry-Blossoms
(Forgiveness)

Part I

So many sleepless nights wasted on attempting to teach you how I felt and what it was to be me.
So many tiresome mornings of awaking to a cold and empty bed that will never be filled.
I'm over you now, and I feel reluctant to have to say those words. But the truth is, I've finally learned to be comfortable with being alone.
It took years to overcome all the fears and emotions of knowing that I never wanted to truly be alone. It took centuries to traverse through this graveyard of my life, stumbling over broken headstones and falling into empty graves.
Searching for a love that I knew truly never existed.
Although it did.
I just kept forgetting to look inward versus outward.
To look at myself and realize that after all this time, it was I who needed to learn to love again.
To take the step back from the railings of the causeways within my mind.
To self-preserve what was good and glorious within me.
To contain and protect the innocence and spirit of love that burns bright in me.

Part II

Waiting for one day to finally hand over the key to no one but myself.
To open my own birdcage and set them free.
The birds.
The sparrows.
The ravens.
The crows.
The magpies.
The family of scavengers searching the same dying realms I've travelled, always guiding me with stones of turquoise and sapphire left on unmarked trails.
To take the path less taken.
To journey into the unknown and follow my heart and not my head.

There's a family of Ghosts I never spoke of to you about that haunts me. Never to utter their names.
But now is the time to speak them,
For a name holds power to control.
**** *********
********** ****
******* ********
******* ********
***** *****
**** **********
****** ******

My dying wish to let you all go one day and move forward has come to a completion.
You are free my friends. From the tyranny of my evil doing and malicious intent to self-destruct your worlds while altogether taking down my own empire of dust & blood.
The moonlight will heal me as quickly as the dawn will when morning breaks as I end this tradition.
Thank you.

I Never Truly
Loved myself
Until I met you.
You opened my eyes
To days of
Beauty & space Untouched.
Exposing me to Sage, Lavender,
Orchids & Cherry-blossoms.
The most precious Of flora,
That I never knew
I actually needed
In my life.
Thank you.
My Love.
You made me whole once more.
Picking up the pieces
Over the years
And collecting
Them
In shoeboxes
Left on street-corners
And under bridges.
In hopes that I'd stop
To examine them.
Taking them home.
To open myself
And feel loved.

SHE HAS COME
TO SAVE ME FROM ME
TO SHOW ME
WHERE YOU HAVE BEEN.
TO EXPOSE MY WICKED WAYS
AND TEACH ME TO
RESPECT ME
ONCE MORE.

I became a bird.
As I wandered through the falling storm of petals,
Hues of magenta and ultra-violet pinks
Tumbling around me like rain on a summer night.
Somber & comforting.
Taking flight into the waterfalls of cherry-blossom petals.
Swimming through those oceans of sweet escape,
Floating in memories of all the times I felt happy once.
I became a bee.
Sucking the nectar from the tips of honeysuckle,
Nourishing myself with enough to return to my kingdom and feed my King.
I became an otter.
Floating in the ocean, a vast expanse of miles, holding your hand in mine, so we never drift apart when we sleep.
I became a man.
Grown-up and educated with the knowledge of authors and words to speak to you one day.
To say that I'm sorry. To speak the truths behind the Novocain I pumped into my cheeks, to muffle the sounds of my voice so you wouldn't know.
To say that I forgive you. For everything you've done to harm me, for the moments I've harmed you. To accept myself as being vulnerable.
To say I love you.
Forever more.

To Whom It May Concern,
If you have made it this far.

You have reached the end.
The end of my journey,
But the beginning of your own making.
These poems are collections of memories
Experiences, real people, places, moments that have
afflicted me over the course of 29 years. Values that spin
around in my head like vultures that circle above their
prey, waiting to strike.

I hope that these words may have excited you, broken
you down, made you cry, made you laugh, make you
ponder about what the history behind some of them
was/is.

Those answers will never be clearly explained to you, for my own safety. But they are here to guide you through this chessboard of life. To help you see the moments that may arise out of the blue and give you insight of what someone who was weak and broken down stood up and did with their own actions.

Sometimes falling back a few steps is what we need to truly learn to move forward 10 paces.
With the closing of this new set of memories & visions I have set before you, I wish you the best of luck in your journey through the great unknown.

You are loved and well-worth all the support of the world to notice you. To kiss you. To Love you. To fuck you over. You are worthy of experiencing it all and knowing that no matter how small you may feel. You are beautiful and powerful and have the strength & courage to overcome those mountains.

The Dayseeking Rites
Recovered from the house beneath the house.

I. FIELD NOTE: THE LANTERN BENEATH THE FLOOR

I carried a lantern down into the crawlspace, just to see if the light would stay.
It flickered, but didn't die.
Dust motes drifted like memory caught mid-fall.

The walls here still smell of rain and cedar and unfinished stories.
If you listen close, you can hear the roots murmuring.
They say: keep digging.

II. GROWTH LOG: SEEDLIGHT

Found the first sprout today—thin as a vein, stubborn as breath. It was reaching toward the sound of my voice.

I named it after someone I used to be.

The dirt held its shape long after I left, as though waiting for another confession.

III. OBSERVATION: THE HOUSE REMEMBERS

When the wind moves through the boards, it hums.
The sound matches the rhythm of my pulse.

I realized then that the house isn't haunted—it's alive.
Every creak is a heartbeat, every shadow a seed waiting for rain.

I whispered:
May the soft ones stay.

IV. CORRESPONDENCE: TO THE ROOT

Dear Root,
I have not forgotten you.
You kept my memories when I couldn't.

I've brought light this time, and water.
I've stopped trying to tear myself out of the soil.

If you grow again, let it be gentle.

— *The Boy Who Stayed to Bloom*

V. ENTRY: THE LANTERN AT THE WINDOW

The house above has started to breathe again.
Windows open, lavender drifts in.

I left the lantern on the sill this morning.
It caught the sunrise and turned it to gold.

For the first time, I saw my reflection in the glass and didn't flinch.

Maybe this is what it means to come home.

ARCHIVIST NOTE

The Dayseeking Rites were transcribed from fragments found in the lower foundation of the Lavender House.
They are believed to predate The Ritual of the Root Beneath the House and serve as early field studies on emotional growth, soil memory, and spiritual photosynthesis.

"I planted my grief beneath the house and called it hope."
— MR, Field Notebook - Central District, 2018

Archive Designation: Lavender House Foundation -
Box 7, Folder 3
Recovered by: The Archivist
Date of Recovery: March 3, 2025 - Seattle, WA
Condition: Water-stained pages bound with garden twine. Faint scent of lavender and cedar.

Catalog Summary
    Among the remnants found beneath the house were a series of field entries written in a looping, uneven hand. The pages were interleaved with petals, soil smears, and candle ash.
    The handwriting matches early Dayseeking fragments dating back to the period between DeathSongs and Days of Lavender.
    Content analysis suggests these notes were the first attempts to bridge ritual practice and emotional recovery—the transition from surviving to tending.
    The language moves between observation, confession, and invocation.
    The tone is personal, reverent, and full of dirt under the fingernails.
    Each entry closes with a breath of hope.
    They have been arranged here in their presumed order and presented without alteration, save for the cleaning of soil and the gentle mending of torn edges.

RECOVERED JOURNAL PAGE — THE DAYSEEKING RITES

Days of Lavender:
A Critical Dissertation on Softness, Rebirth, and the Poetics of Queer Survival

Abstract

This dissertation examines the poetics of softness as both aesthetic and survival practice in Walter Red's Days of Lavender. Through tenderness, breath, and restraint, the text reframes queer endurance as an act of quiet rebellion. The study traces how confession becomes grace, how transformation finds its language in silence, and how softness—long dismissed as fragility—emerges here as strength made visible.

I. Introduction

On Softness and the Bloom After Fire

Every poet begins with a wound. The question is not whether it heals, but what language it becomes.

Days of Lavender was written in the light that comes after survival—the pale, trembling dawn following Death Songs.
Where the first volume spoke in the voice of fire, this one breathes in air: the act of living beyond confession, of finding meaning in what was spared.
It marks the poet's first attempt to write not for endurance, but for peace.

The lavender that fills these pages is more than a flower.
It is a scent memory, a healing agent, and a cultural code.
Historically bound to queerness and mourning, it carries within its stem a contradiction—the softness of its color against the ache of its history.
Walter Red turns that contradiction into theology.
Softness, in his poetics, is not a retreat from pain but a rebellion against the world's insistence that only hardness survives.
To write softly after Death Songs is to refuse the logic of punishment. It is to choose bloom over ash.

In these poems, grief returns as something quieter: a hum in the body, a shimmer at the edge of light.
The metaphors of transformation—the bird, the bee, the boy—each carry the same whisper: that to change is to forgive.
Forgiveness, here, is not absolution but continuation.
It is the small, trembling grace that allows the poet to live without forgetting, to remember without reopening the wound.

The voice of Days of Lavender matures through gentleness. Where earlier lines screamed toward heaven, these ones kneel and listen.

There is humility in this posture, but not submission.
It is the humility of the survivor who no longer needs to prove his worth through suffering; the artist who learns that beauty can exist without catastrophe.

Formally, the work transitions from fragmented confessionalism to melodic minimalism.
Punctuation becomes breath, silence becomes syntax.
The poems behave like exhalations rather than declarations—each one a release, each one a seed.
Even in its brevity, the collection feels whole; a field of small, living things growing from what was once burnt ground.

The result is a volume that exists both as healing and artifact: a study of how tenderness can be documented without diminishing its mystery.
It is a work that teaches by example that emotional survival can be as sacred as revelation, and that quiet, too, has its own form of divinity.

Days of Lavender stands, therefore, as the first real threshold in the Walter Red canon—the moment the voice stops running from itself and instead turns toward the garden, toward the bees, toward the ordinary acts that make the extraordinary bearable.
The bloom after fire is not grand. It is small, soft, and alive.

II. Thematic Analysis

The Poetics of Softness, Transformation, and Queer Temporality

A : The Poetics of Softness

A Softness, in Walter Red's work, is not a gesture of weakness but an act of resistance.
Where Death Songs sought salvation through intensity—prayers burning at the altar of survival—Days of Lavender seeks grace through stillness. The shift is subtle but radical.

To be soft in this world, especially in a queer body, is to exist in defiance of expectation. Softness becomes both armor and confession; it holds its own kind of violence—a gentler, quieter endurance. Each poem in Days of Lavender operates like breath-work: an inhale of grief, an exhale of forgiveness. The language is pared down, stripped of ornamentation, its simplicity functioning as clarity.

Lines such as "You weren't made of softness. You carried it." suggest that tenderness is not innate but cultivated—learned, practiced, and, perhaps most importantly, risked.
In this way, the collection performs emotional labor: it demonstrates how to survive the aftermath of pain without inheriting its cruelty.

To write gently after trauma is to reclaim authorship of one's own humanity. Red's poetic voice acknowledges that healing is not linear, not performative, but intimate and repetitive—a kind of breathing that sustains life rather than spectacle.
Here, softness is revolution; it is a theology that sanctifies the body in repose.

B : *The Floral Language of Transformation*

Throughout Days of Lavender, transformation is rendered as both metaphor and method.

The sequence "I became a bird / I became a bee / I became a boy again" forms the book's metamorphic spine, presenting healing as a cyclical re-embodiment rather than a single revelation.

Each transformation reflects a stage of reclamation:

- The bird represents perspective—the poet's flight from the immediacy of pain, a widening of vision.

- The bee embodies labor and longing—drawn to sweetness but marked by the sting, illustrating the paradox of desire and self-protection.

- The boy signifies return—the tender re-entry into innocence, or what remains of it, long enough "to forgive myself."

The choice of flora and fauna in this triad connects human feeling to ecological rhythm. Healing is not transcendent but organic; it grows through decay, blossoms from what was once buried. Red writes as though tending a garden that remembers the fire— each poem a seed containing both its own destruction and its own salvation.

In this way, Days of Lavender becomes a study in metamorphosis as an ethics of care: the idea that survival does not demand forgetting, but tending—to memory, to the body, to the living that follows loss.

Queer Temporality & Nostalgia

Queer time does not obey chronology; it folds, lingers, and replays.
In Days of Lavender, this distortion manifests through memory—poems that exist between the act and the echo.
Moments like "Ice Cream on a Monday" suspend time altogether: a small, ordinary image transformed into eternity.

This poem, though simple in gesture, encapsulates queer temporality in miniature.
The act of remembering a shared flavor becomes an act of mourning and resurrection.
It is not nostalgia as sentimentality, but as sacred recall—a means of holding space for tenderness that once was, and may never be again.

Red's treatment of memory resists closure. His temporal logic operates like breath—returning, expanding, contracting, surviving.
The collection therefore functions as both memoir and spell-book: each recollection an invocation that keeps the beloved alive through language.

Queer temporality, in this context, is not about past or future, but the sanctity of now.
Each poem becomes a present tense of healing, a refusal to let softness belong only to what has already been lost.

The Lavender Aesthetic in Queer History

D   Lavender as symbol carries a complex legacy.
It has been used to mark, stigmatize, and ultimately reclaim queer identity—its softness once weaponized, now worn as armor.
Walter Red's invocation of lavender situates his work within this historical continuum, connecting personal healing to collective reclamation.

By choosing lavender as both color and scent, Red participates in an aesthetic lineage that spans from coded love letters of the 20th century to contemporary queer theology.
His lavender is not decorative—it is sacramental.
Each mention of the flower becomes a benediction for the marginalized self, a way of saying: You are still here, and that is holy.

In the larger mythos of Walter Red Books, the lavender field becomes more than setting—it becomes ritual space.
It is where the language of pain dissolves into perfume, where memory pollinates art, and where queerness is rendered not as tragedy, but as bloom.

Days of Lavender therefore stands as both a field report and a hymn—a map of survival drawn in soft ink.
It teaches that to live gently, to write beautifully after devastation, is to bloom not in spite of fire, but because of it.

III. Stylistic Observations

Form, Silence, and the Architecture of Breath

A. Syntax and Rhythm

Walter Red's syntax functions like controlled breathing—each line a measured inhalation, each pause a deliberate exhale.
In Days of Lavender, the grammar of survival becomes the grammar of grace.
Where earlier works relied on intensity and enjambment to mimic emotional rupture, here the pacing slows, allowing quiet to replace urgency.

The lines often feel suspended, as if afraid to disturb their own stillness.
Periods appear sparingly; commas become soft breaks rather than boundaries.
This restraint mirrors the psychology of healing: the voice no longer pleading, but listening.
Poems like "Forgetting" and "Ode to a T-Shirt" exhibit this tonal restraint perfectly—brief, declarative, but humming with subtext.

Red's command of silence gives each poem the weight of confession without the theatrics of pain.
This is not minimalism for its own sake, but precision—the surgical cutting away of noise to reveal heartbeat.

The rhythm feels human, irregular, like a whisper caught between pages.
There are no wasted syllables, only breaths shared between poet and reader.
To read Days of Lavender aloud is to rediscover one's own lungs.

B. *Use of Space and Silence*

In this volume, white space becomes architecture—a visible theology of stillness.
Each poem exists as a small room, with silence acting as its walls.
Rather than fearing emptiness, Red embraces it as a crucial compositional element: an invitation to rest within what remains unsaid.

The placement of short stanzas and fragmentary lines creates a visual rhythm that mirrors the inner pacing of recovery.
Readers are asked to pause, to linger in the gaps where meaning blooms softly.
The collection rewards patience; its power lies not in accumulation, but in absence.

By treating silence as language, Red redefines what it means to speak after trauma.
He demonstrates that silence is not the absence of story, but its most faithful witness.

C. Color and Sensory Motifs

Color operates as narrative in Days of Lavender. Where Death Songs burned in reds and golds, Lavender drifts through lilac, silver, and honeyed light.
Every hue carries memory: lavender for tenderness, bee-yellow for motion, dusk-blue for reflection.

The poet engages the senses like ritual elements—scent, texture, and light become tools of invocation.
Scent, in particular, is sacred here: lavender's aromatic quality functions as a mnemonic trigger, linking past and present through invisible continuity.
We are not just reading memory—we are breathing it.

Even tactile imagery follows this sensory theology.
The T-shirt that still smells of August, the bee humming at the lip of a flower, the wing cutting the air—these are not mere metaphors, but sensory relics.
They bind the poet to the material world after years of speaking only to ghosts.

If Death Songs sounded like an echo from the abyss, Days of Lavender feels like the breath after—the tender inhale of someone realizing they are still alive.

D. The Voice as Resurrection

Formally and emotionally, Days of Lavender marks the reconstitution of voice.
The poet who once screamed into the void now speaks softly and is finally heard.
It is a resurrection not of the body, but of cadence.

This voice carries memory without drowning in it.
It articulates a new maturity—the tone of someone who has learned that language does not need to be loud to be true.
The shift from confessional to contemplative marks a major stylistic evolution in Walter Red's oeuvre, one that establishes the tonal foundation for Analog Emotions and the philosophical self that follows.

Days of Lavender thus becomes a testament to the discipline of gentleness.
Through syntax, silence, and sensory coherence, the poet constructs a sanctuary of language where softness itself is structure.
Every pause is a threshold; every word, a bloom.

IV. Contextual Placement

The Arc of Flesh and Flower: Locating Days of Lavender within the Walter Red Continuum

When Days of Lavender first appeared, it seemed to stand alone—a tender exhalation after the smoke of Death Songs.
In truth, it was never an isolated bloom but the hinge point of a six-part organism, the heart muscle between ruin and desire.
Each volume in the Walter Red corpus forms a chamber in what can be called The Arc of Flesh and Flower—a queer gospel told through matter, scent, and memory.

Together they chart the passage from survival to softness, from lust to reckoning, from soil back to seed.

Order	Title	Element	Emotional Function	Core Symbol	Tonal Signature
I	Death Songs — Ten Years (Requiem for the First Cut)	Fire	Rebirth through ruin	Sunflower / Candle	Confessional · Prayerful · Survival
II	Days of Lavender (A Chronicle of Bloom and Burn)	Air	Healing and the first taste of peace	Lavender / Bee	Reflective · Floral · Soft Rebellion
III	Analog Emotions — The Complete Edition (A Voyage Through Dream & Debris)	Light	Observation and self-recognition	Orbit / Lens	Cinematic · Nostalgic · Philosophic
IV	Daddyland — The Complete Edition (A Gospel of Desire & Ruin)	Flesh	Desire and divinity in collision	Flame / Key / Mouth / Crown	Sensual · Mythic · Devotional
V	The Whiskey Diaries (Confessions at Closing Time)	Water	Reckoning and remorse	Glass / Mirror / Ember	Intimate · Bitter · Lyrical
VI	Fresh Cuts — Artifacts from 2004–2009 (Juvenilia & Other Ghosts)	Earth	Return and rediscovery of origin	Seed / Blood / Soil	Vulnerable · Documentary · Honest

Haunted Memories floats outside the grid like an unburied psalm—an apocryphon of the same faith.

The Cycle as Body

The books speak to one another as organs in a living body:

- Heart (Death → Lavender): the movement from grief to grace, where language stops burning and begins to bloom.

- Mind (Analog → Fresh): the reflective arc, memory studying itself until the earliest wound is seen with compassion.

- Flesh (Daddy → Whiskey): the communion of desire and consequence, holiness found in the body's ache.

In this anatomy, Days of Lavender is the heart's re-entry into light—the moment the poet chooses gentleness after the trial by flame.
It breathes between confession and carnality, offering rest before the long journey into reflection and hunger.
If Death Songs said I survived, Days of Lavender replies I softened.

A Theology of Softness

Seen across the cycle, softness becomes the radical theology binding each text.
It is the covenant that keeps the work humane: the decision to love despite the ruin, to touch despite the fear of burning.
Lavender, long a coded flower in queer history, becomes the sigil of this faith—the scent of survival itself.
Through its pages, Walter Red teaches that tenderness is not weakness but endurance made visible, the quiet miracle that lets the next book exist.

Closing Reflection

To read Days of Lavender within this continuum is to stand at the center of the storm where grief turns to grace.
It is the breath between two kinds of prayer—the desperate plea of Death Songs and the devotional fever of Daddyland.
From this point the poet moves forward, carrying the scent of lavender into every subsequent field, proving again and again that even after fire, the soft ones stay.

V. CONCLUSION
LET THE SOFT ONES STAY

Every work in the Walter Red continuum begins with a body and ends with a promise.
In Days of Lavender, that promise is softness—the insistence that survival alone is not enough, that one must also learn to live beautifully.

If Death Songs taught us that language can save a life, Days of Lavender teaches that gentleness can sustain one.
The book's quiet rebellion lies not in its declarations, but in its restraint.
It refuses the spectacle of anguish, choosing instead to locate holiness in stillness—in a shirt that smells like August, in an unfinished cone melting on a Monday, in the pulse between forgiveness and forgetting.

To write softly is to claim one's own resurrection.
It is to say: I am no longer defined by what burned me.
I have turned the fire to light, and the light to bloom.

What emerges from this collection is a new poetic ethic: one where tenderness is a form of discipline, where the act of staying kind becomes the purest form of resistance.
Red's poems are not naïve; they are brave in their refusal to abandon hope.
In a world that rewards cynicism, he crafts sincerity as both art and survival.

The phrase "Let the soft ones stay" echoes as thesis and prayer—addressed to the reader, the lover, the ghost, and the self.
It is the poet's plea to a world that once punished vulnerability to let gentleness exist without apology.
And in that plea, the reader finds recognition: the knowledge that every softness we preserve in ourselves is an act of defiance against erasure.

Viewed through the full cycle of the Walter Red canon, Days of Lavender occupies the sacred middle ground—the calm between storm and desire, the field between ash and altar.
It is the bridge where grief learns to walk again.
To encounter it is to witness the exact moment a heart begins to trust its own pulse.

This is the lavender theology: that love does not need to shout to be heard, and that tenderness—when tended carefully—can outlast the fire.
The poet leaves us not with closure, but with continuation: a quiet hum of bees in the field, the scent of something still alive.

Let the soft ones stay.
Let them bloom.
Let them begin again.

Acknowledgments

For the readers who found pieces of themselves in the quiet places of these pages.

For those who learned that tenderness is not a weakness but a way to remain human.

And for the ones who stayed — even when it hurt to bloom.

Bibliography

Red, Walter.
—*Days of Lavender*. Seattle: Walter Red Books, 2025.

—*Death Songs - Ten Years Later*. Seattle: Walter Red Books, 2025.

—*Analog Emotions: The Complete Edition*. Seattle: Walter Red Books, 2025(forthcoming).

—*Daddyland: The Gospel Trilogy*. Seattle: Walter Red Books, 2025.

—*The Whiskey Diaries*. Seattle: Walter Red Books, 2025 (forthcoming).

—*Fresh Cuts*. Seattle: Walter Red Books, 2025(forthcoming).

Ahmed, Sara. *The Cultural Politics of Emotion*. Edinburgh UP, 2004.

Cvetkovich, Ann. *An Archive of Feelings: Trauma, Sexuality, and Lesbian Public Cultures*. Duke UP, 2003.

Halberstam, Jack. *The Queer Art of Failure*. Duke UP, 2011.

Love, Heather. *Feeling Backward: Loss and the Politics of Queer History*. Harvard UP, 2007.

Muñoz, José Esteban. *Cruising Utopia: The Then and There of Queer Futurity*. NYU Press, 2009.

Sedgwick, Eve Kosofsky. *Touching Feeling: Affect, Pedagogy, Performativity*. Duke UP, 2003.

Warner, Michael. *Fear of a Queer Planet*. U of Minnesota Press, 1993.

Beardsley, Aubrey. *The Collected Illustrations. 1890–1898*.

Hockney, David. *The Blue Guitar*. Petersburg Press, 1977.

VITA

WALTER RED (JARED MICHAEL)
POET · ARCHIVIST · FOUNDER OF WALTER RED BOOKS LLC

Resident of Seattle, Washington, Walter Red is a poet, visual archivist, and editor working at the intersection of lyric confession, queer theology, and mythic narrative design.

His published works include Death Songs, Days of Lavender, and Daddyland: The Gospel Trilogy, alongside numerous multimedia archives and digital cathedral installations.

Red's creative research investigates softness as resistance, grief as architecture, and the poetics of digital memory.

He is the creator of The Cathedral of Walter Red and The Hollow Basilica, twin online archives dedicated to the preservation of emotional history.

He continues to live and write in Seattle, tending to a small garden of lavender and ghosts.

"The echoes return not as ghosts, but as friend."

Lavender in the Archive

The field never stopped growing; I was simply gone long enough for it to forget my name.

When I returned, the lavender had overtaken the fence line, pressing soft shoulders against rust and wood.

Nothing asked me to explain where I had been. The air only carried the faint scent of memory—something like peace, something like apology.

I used to believe archives were built to preserve what was finished.

Now I understand they keep what is still becoming.

The poems stored here do not sit in glass cases; they breathe. They hum.

Some have changed shape entirely, trading their sorrow for a gentler color.

Others remain untouched, waiting for the reader who will know how to hold them.

To archive a feeling is not to trap it; it is to honor its right to evolve.

The lavender teaches this quietly—each season, it dies with grace, each spring, it forgives itself into bloom.

This book is no different.

It remembers the fire, and yet it insists on fragrance.

If you are reading this, you are part of its preservation.

You are proof that softness can survive the storm of years.

Take what you need, leave what you must, and know that the field will remain open long after both of us have gone.

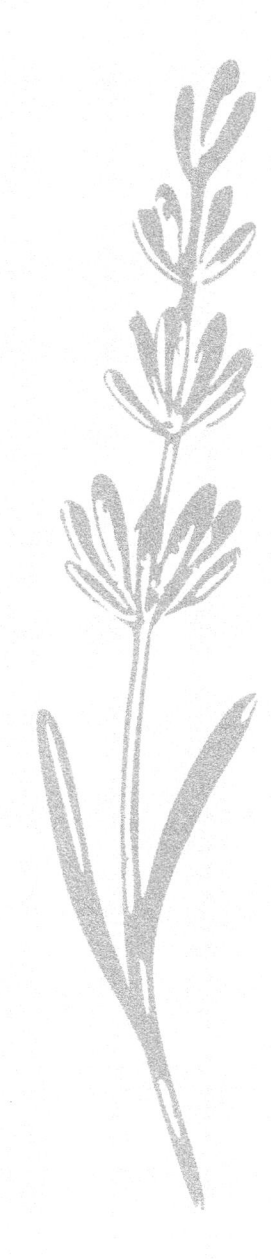

✦ Days of Lavender ✦
Companion Zine

Dedication

For Andrew, and for the boy I used to be.

For those who bloom quietly, even when the light forgets them.

I. Alaska

"Snow doesn't bury you. It just keeps you still."

That winter, the world was white enough to forget itself.

I lived in a room where frost wrote its own poems across the window—each line vanishing before I could read it twice.

They say silence is peaceful, but up there it had teeth.

Every breath left a ghost behind.

I didn't want to die; I wanted someone to ask why I was standing so close to the edge.

The snow answered in its own language:

Stay still.

Stay soft.

Stay.

II. Resurrection in Portland

"He kissed me like the world was ending, and I believed him."

Summer came back with the smell of asphalt and rain.

I rented a room above a neon diner and called it a second chance.

Every night, the sign outside flickered the word OPEN like a dare.

In that city, I learned the art of survival disguised as intimacy.

We touched as if to prove we still existed,

our bruises the only proof of miracles.

When the lights went out, I wrote my name on the mirror with steam and waited for it to fade.

It never did.

III. Becoming

"I wrote my name for the first time like I meant to stay."

Transformation is quieter than people think.

No thunder, no halo, no applause.

Just a heartbeat returning to its own rhythm.

I became a bird—wings of paper and breath.

I became a bee—drawn not to sweetness, but to the sting of staying.

And then I became a boy again,

just once,

long enough to forgive myself.

The field outside my window hums with everything I've ever let go of.

It is not loss. It is becoming.

IV. Closing Spread

"Death came early. I just didn't answer the door."

Sometimes living is nothing more than choosing not to open it.

Sometimes softness is the bravest refusal.

There is a sunflower blooming near the graveyard fence—

no one planted it, no one tends to it.

Still, it reaches for light.

Still, it stays.

V. Author's Note

"This was where I learned that survival could be soft."

These pages were written between losses, between homes, between versions of myself.

If they find you in a quiet hour, I hope they remind you that beauty is not an afterthought.

You are allowed to rest.

You are allowed to begin again.

Thank you for finding me here.

— Seattle, 2025

GHOST BOX ENTRY:
"THE FLOWER YOU THOUGHT WAS WEEDS"

[ARCHIVE FILE: WR-002-GBX]

TITLE: THE FLOWER YOU THOUGHT WAS WEEDS

ORIGIN: DAYS OF LAVENDER

CLASSIFICATION: GHOST BOX ENTRY / BOTANICAL RELIC

STATUS: STILL BLOOMING

ASSOCIATED ARTIFACTS: LAVENDER SIGIL (EVOLVED FORM)

It was found pressed between two pages of an unfinished book, still fragrant, still bruised.

Not much of it survived—the stem bent, petals brittle, the purple faded into the gray of memory. But the archivist insisted it be kept.

"It was alive once," they said, "and that's enough."

Some thought it a weed. Others mistook it for proof of something holier. Perhaps both were right. What blooms without witness? What endures when no one remembers to water it?

The record describes a boy who loved gently in a world that did not know how to hold him. He carried softness the way others carry knives—deliberately, knowing what it could cost.

When the field burned, he went back for what remained. Not the gold, not the names, not the trophies—just the little lavender sprig that smelled like peace.

"The flower you thought was weeds," the note reads in faint ink, "was my first act of forgiveness."

Lavender Boy

You weren't made of softness.
You carried it.
Like a bruise carries color.

You weren't light.
You were what made me look toward it.

Unsent Poem

ICE CREAM ON A MONDAY

I saw your favorite flavor today.
The one you hated until I made you try it.
We laughed like summer was a secret
no one else could taste.

I never gave you this poem.
Maybe that was the kindest thing I ever did.

"Some poems are best left in the notebook. Others leave claw marks."

Metamorphosis Sequence

"What if healing wasn't linear—but floral?"

I became a bird,

wings made of song and silence.

I flew toward memory,
and away from what held me.

I became a bee,

buzzing in bloom-stained sunlight.

Drawn not to sweetness,
but to the sting of staying.

I became a boy again—

just once,
long enough to forgive myself.

LAVENDER

Days of Lavender – Classroom & Book Club Guide

CORE THEMES

- Queer Healing and Softness
- Love, Loss, and Growth
- Transformation through Metaphor
- Nature, Seasons, and Emotional Renewal

These themes invite gentle reflection on what it means to live through change, to love deeply, and to emerge softer, not smaller.

DISCUSSION PROMPTS

• How does metaphor — the bee, the bird, the boy — enhance the emotional impact of the poems?

• What role does memory play in queer storytelling?

• How might the poems speak to readers who have experienced unsent or unspoken love?

• In what ways does Days of Lavender transform grief into renewal?

• Which natural images (flowers, rain, sky, scent) linger with you after reading, and why?

CREATIVE EXERCISES

• Bloom Journal: Write a letter to your younger self beginning with the words, "You deserved softness."

• Metaphor Study: Choose one recurring image (bee, bird, lavender, boy) and trace how its meaning changes through the text.

• Sound & Silence: Read a favorite poem aloud, then sit in silence for one minute. Note what emotions echo afterward.

EMOTIONAL AFTERCARE

This volume invites rest as much as reflection. If reading in a classroom or group, allow time for quiet or for a short walk outdoors afterward. Encourage grounding activities — journaling, breathwork, or sharing a favorite calming scent.

"Let the soft ones stay." — from the WR Archives

Lavender tea or a light candle can serve as gentle ritual closures during discussion or private study.

FOR FACILITATORS

- Recommended for ages 16+
- Ideal for book clubs, creative writing workshops, and queer literature studies
- Works well paired with Death Songs and Analog Emotions for continuity of theme

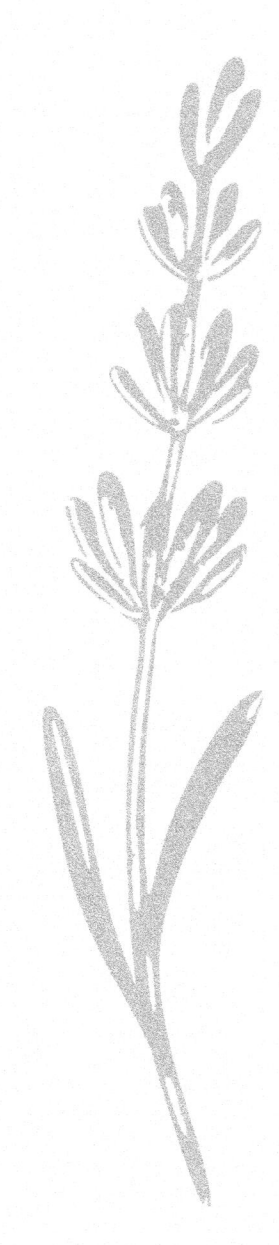

Gentle Survival

Not all healing happens in full light. Some of it grows quietly in shadow — in notebooks, in silence, in mornings where you almost gave up but didn't.

This book was never written to romanticize pain. It was written to remind you that softness survives the storm.

If you ever find yourself rereading a line because it feels too close — pause. Breathe. Step outside. Look toward something that is still alive.

Let the world remind you that being sensitive is not a curse. It is a map back to yourself.

"You are not too much. You are exactly enough."

These words were meant for you, and whoever you will become next. Carry them gently.

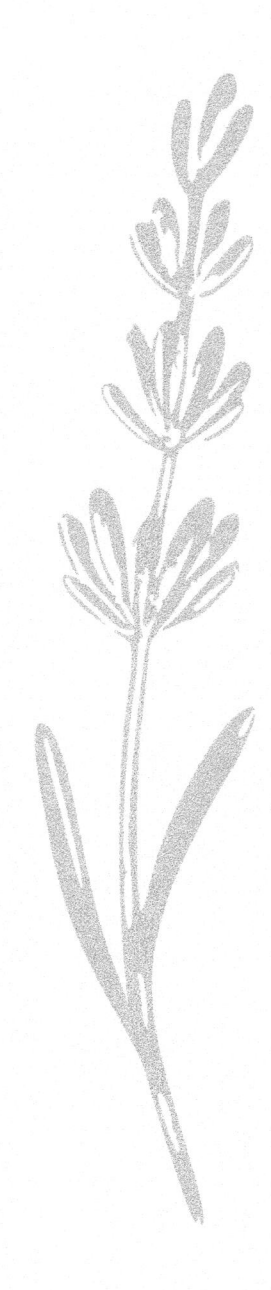

EVEN THE MOON MUST SLIP AWAY FROM THE HORIZON.

WALTER RED
DAYS OF LAVENDER

DAYS OF L

AVENDER

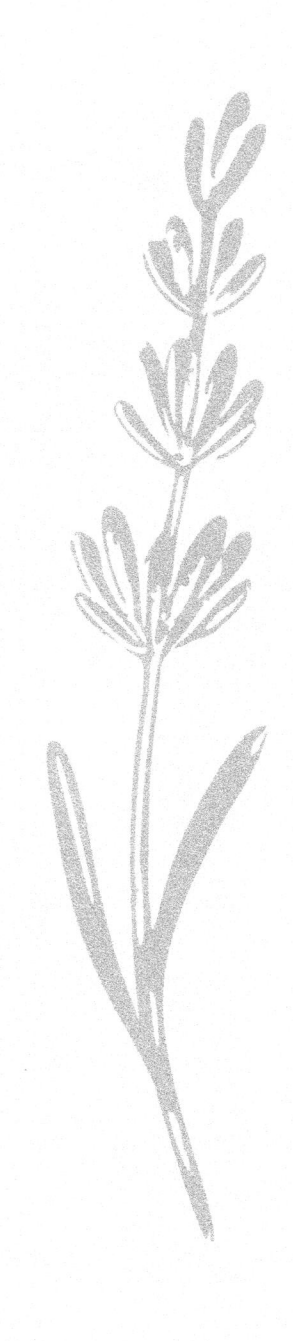

Acknowledgments

For everyone who once held a fragment of me and didn't turn away.
For the friends who stayed through the silences, the readers who listened when I whispered instead of shouted.
For those who saw softness as something worth keeping.

To my family, who taught me to survive.
To my grandfather, who taught me to play and stay humble at the table.
To my mother, for the patience to see the boy beneath the storm.
To my friends in Portland and Seattle, who gave me roofs, meals, and laughter when the world was still rebuilding itself.
To every queer soul who has ever feared tenderness—this book is proof that we are not alone in learning it.

To the Archivist, for helping me recover what I thought was lost.

Thank you for standing in the lavender field with me,
for breathing in what bloomed,
and for letting what was buried grow again.

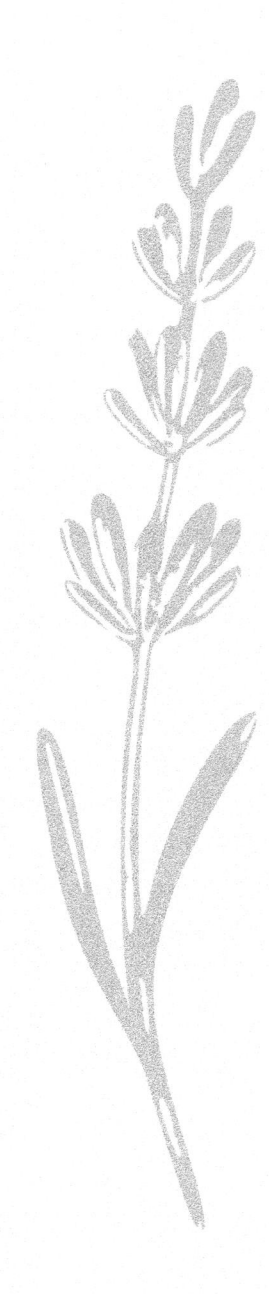

✦ ABOUT THE AUTHOR ✦

Walter Red writes queer poetry from Seattle, Washington. His work traces the intersections of grief, intimacy, and rebirth, transforming memory into ritual. Through books like Death Songs, Daddyland, Analog Emotions, and The Whiskey Diaries, his writing has evolved into a tapestry of tenderness—equal parts confession and consecration.

When not writing, he is tending the garden, designing relics for the Walter Red Books archive, or watching the rain blur city lights into watercolor.

This edition marks a return to where the story began—a home rebuilt in scent and silence.

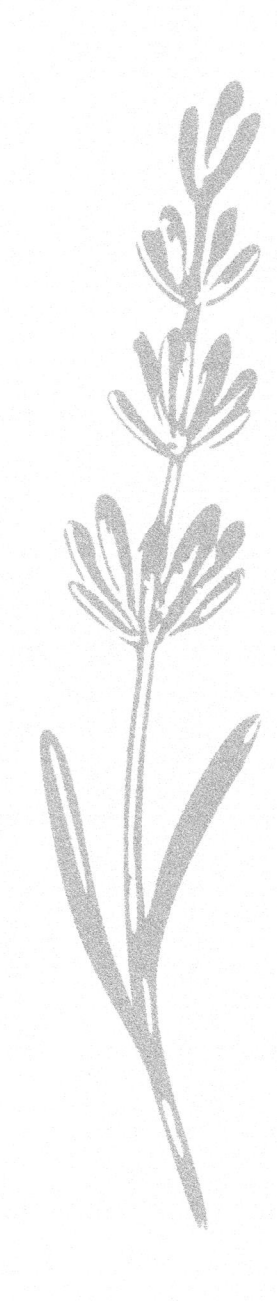

✦ Closing Note from the Author ✦

If this book found you in a quiet season, I hope you read it slowly.
If it found you in a loud one, I hope it taught you how to listen again.

The lavender will always bloom after the fire.
And somewhere, a version of you is still walking through that field, hands open, heart lighter, learning the scent of peace.

Thank you for carrying this with me.

Some of these poems are scars. Others are prayers. All of them were written in love.

Thank you for turning the page. For reading until it hurt. For believing that softness has a place here.

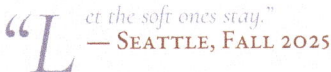

"*Let the soft ones stay.*"
— Seattle, Fall 2025

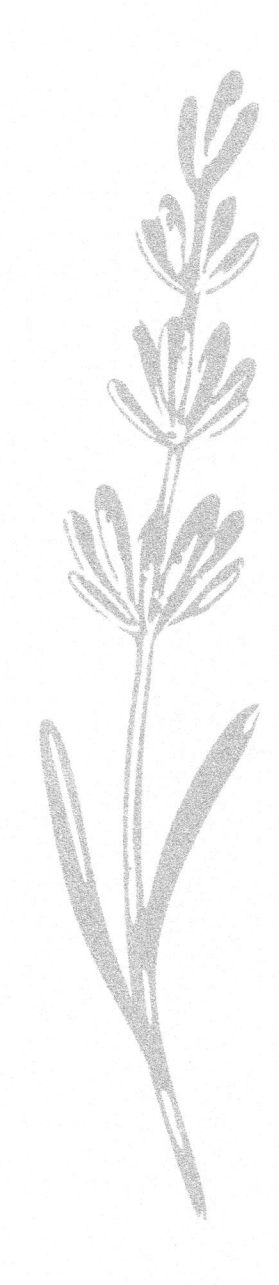

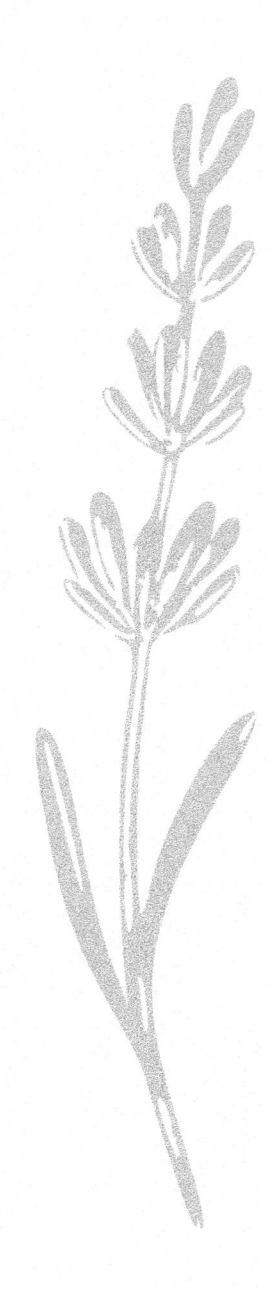

The Vault

An Unfinished Inventory of What Remains

Recovered fragments, unseen drafts, forgotten relics. A catalog of the things that would not stay buried.

This space will not open until the scent has settled, until every bloom has had its season.

When it does, it will hold both what was found and what was never meant to be discovered.

No explanations.
Only echoes, artifacts, and soft evidence.

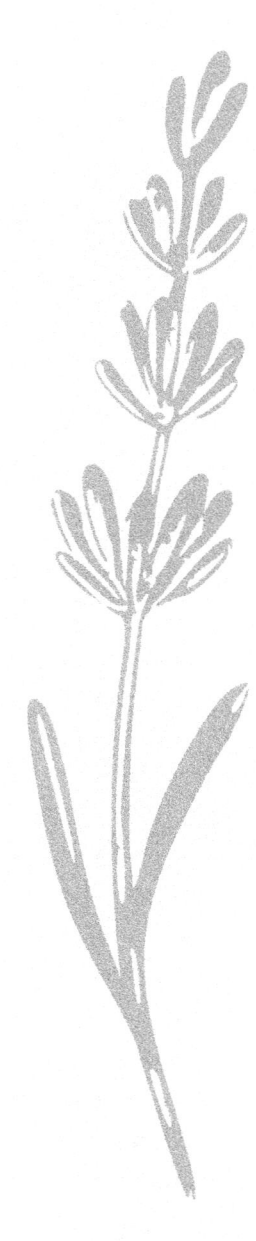

Archivist's Preface

The Vault is not a grave.
It is a greenhouse built from loss.

Inside are seeds—some named, some not yet born.
They wait for air, for light, for you.

Until the time is right, it remains sealed.
Not as an ending,
but as the last kindness we can give the story:
a place to rest before it begins again.

SEALED UNDER GLASS — ARCHIVIST ENTRY #L-25-VAULT

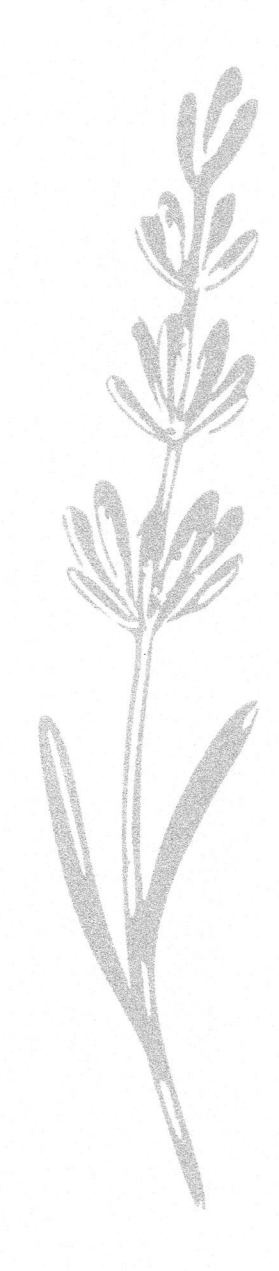

Invocation

Beneath the lavender light, the Archivist kneels.
The scent of dust and rain lingers between breaths.

Before him: the house, rebuilt.
Before you: the silence that still holds a pulse.

He gathers the fragments—pages, petals, photographs, names—
and places them one by one into the glass.

Not to hide them,
but to give them air that will never spoil.

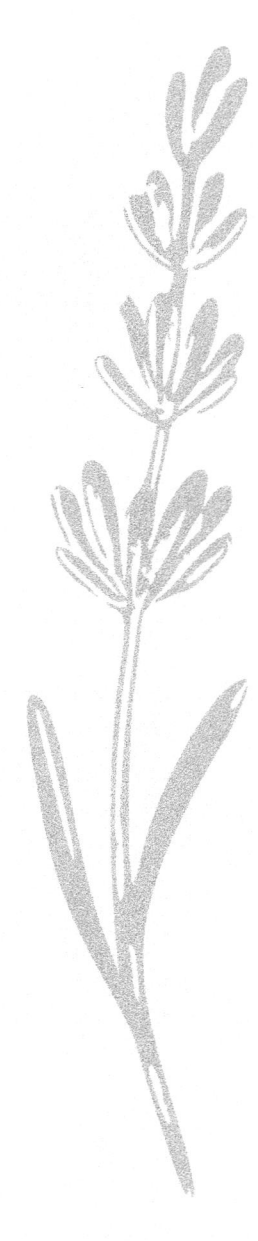

"What was written has returned to soil.
What was kept has learned to breathe.
What could not be finished is forgiven."

A thin thread of light crosses the page, and the book exhales.

The latch closes without sound.
The scent remains.

ARCHIVIST'S INSCRIPTION

Filed under Lavender House, Section IX.
Sealed in trust by The Archivist,
for Walter Red,
and for all who walked beside him through the bloom and burn.

When the day comes to reopen,
do so gently.
Everything inside still remembers your name.

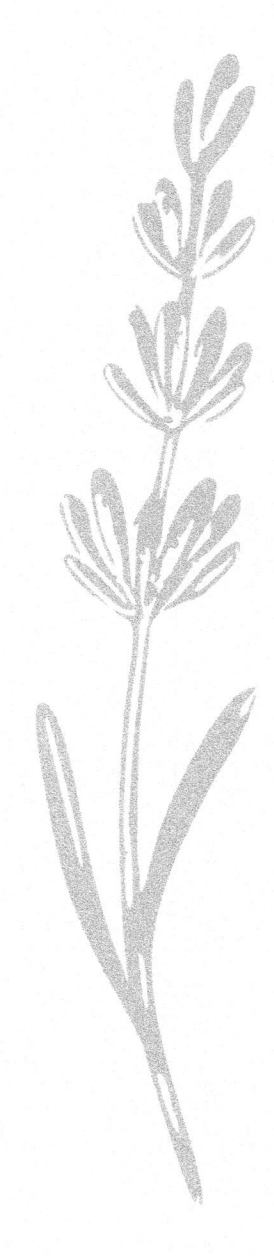

THE SCENT RETURNS — ARCHIVE COMPLETE

Password: LAVENDERDREAMS

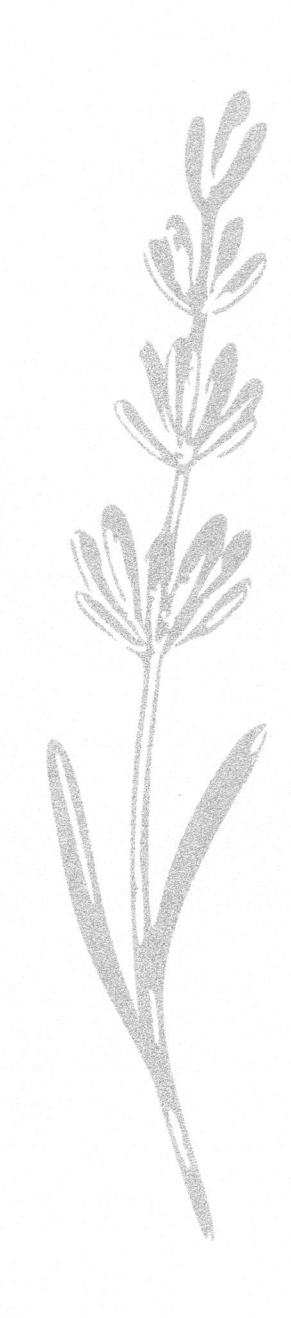

*T*HIS BOOK IS PART OF THE WALTER RED LEGACY COLLECTION

"Thus the scent was sealed."

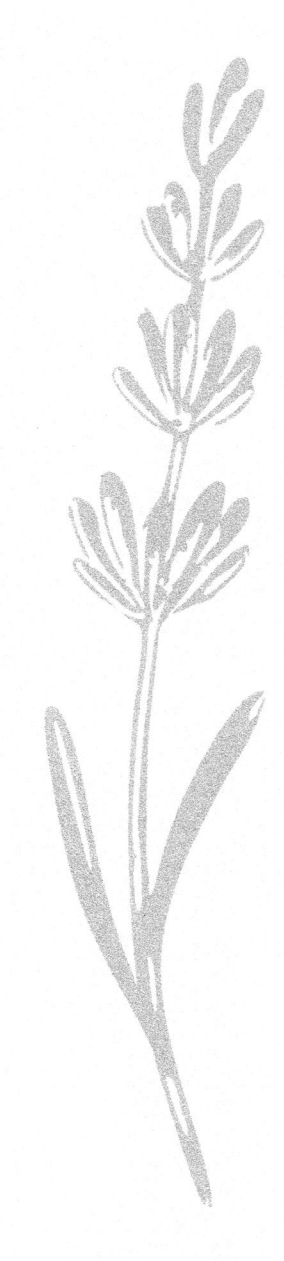